KABBALISTIC
Astrology

Kabbalah Centre Publishing is a registered DBA of
Kabbalah Centre International, Inc.

For further information:

The Kabbalah Centre
1062 S. Robertson Blvd., Los Angeles, CA 90035
155 E. 48th St., New York, NY 10017

1.800.Kabbalah www.kabbalah.com

Printed in USA, May 2019

ISBN: 978-1-57189-556-1
eISBN: 978-1-57189-714-5

Design: HL Design (Hyun Min Lee) www.hldesignco.com

KABBALISTIC

Astrology

And the Meaning of Our Lives

KABBALAH
CENTRE
PUBLISHING

www.kabbalah.com™

RAV BERG

For my wife Karen,
in the vastness of cosmic space
and the infinity of lifetimes,
it is my bliss to share a soul mate
and Age of Aquarius with you.

CONTENTS

ACRUX

BETA CRUCIS

AGENA

RIGIL K

SPICA

ANTARES

INTRODUCTION

K abbalah is a universal technology, the world's most ancient tradition of secret knowledge. From the very first days of Creation, it was passed directly from the Creator to Adam, Abraham, Sarah, Rachel, Moses, and the other biblical patriarchs and matriarchs. Kabbalah predates any religion or secular organization. It is the heritage and birthright of all humanity.

Literally translated, the Aramaic word *Kabbalah* means "to receive." Kabbalah is the study of what receiving really means on both the spiritual and practical levels of existence. Kabbalah reveals how things happen and, more importantly, *why* things happen in all areas of our lives, even in the dimensions beyond our physical existence.

Although kabbalists speak of the Upper Worlds, Kabbalah does not envision heaven as somewhere up in the sky. Paradise is defined by heightened spiritual power and awareness, not by altitude. The Light of the Creator is everywhere

—in ourselves and in other human beings, in trees and in animals, even in inanimate objects. Our purpose in life, therefore, is not to call down the Light from heaven above, but to kindle the sparks of Light that are already here. Kabbalah requires no religious training or indoctrination to make that happen. Connecting with the Light is something we can do right now.

Literally everything we do is a chance to achieve that purpose. Reading these words at this moment is an especially important opportunity. If this book is your first introduction to Kabbalah, you are about to gain some powerful tools for improving your life and the lives of everyone you meet. If you are already familiar with the wisdom of Kabbalah, the chapters that follow will provide both practical knowledge and spiritual insights to deepen your understanding.

No matter who you are or why you have chosen to open this book, the ancient wisdom of Kabbalah is a gift from the Creator to you and all humanity. This book was created to help you enjoy that gift to the fullest.

ACRUX

BETA CRUCIS

AGENA

RIGIL K

SPICA

ANTARES

Section I:

BLUEPRINT OF
A HUMAN SOUL

DNA OF THE SOUL

A quick question for our male readers: Do you remember the exact moment as a kid when your voice suddenly cracked and you found yourself speaking in a tone many octaves lower than the day before?

Do you remember the precise moment when the clear, smooth skin on your face suddenly broke out in blemishes? You had to begin applying acne cream and washing with expensive, deep-cleansing soap.

We might not recall the month, day, or moment when such things occurred, but this information was already known and recorded in the DNA of our cells. It was preset in our genes at the moment we arrived in this world.

That also goes for the color of our hair, the size of our waists, and our predisposition toward the various ailments that can afflict us during the course of our lives. All of our physical traits and characteristics are determined and governed by our

genes. It is the information encoded in the DNA that determines the characteristics of all living things.

DNA is a genetic "language" formed with its own alphabet.
In the late 1950s, biologists cracked the code of life and discovered the genetic alphabet, which is composed of four "letters"—ATCG. ATCG refers to four different kinds of
nucleotides that translate into 20 amino acids, the building
blocks of proteins. Protein molecules are what make you and
me "living stuff."

The four nucleotides combine to create "words" and "sen-
tences" that compose the genetic code of an individual. Each
person has about three billion combination of "letters" in his
or her genetic code. The differences among people lie in the
combination and sequences of their four nucleotide "letters."

All we really are, therefore, is a set of living chemical symbols.
We are all alphabetic in structure.

In the same way that the physical body contains DNA, so too
does the human soul. Just as cellular DNA determines the
development of our physical bodies throughout our lifetime,
the DNA of our souls determines our spiritual and emotional
development. Even more remarkable, our spiritual DNA is
also expressed through letters, as we will discover shortly.

Our genetic programming is inherited from our parents.
Mom's and Dad's various physical attributes are passed down
to us, recorded in our genetic code. But how do we acquire

the spiritual DNA in our souls? Where does it come from? How do we know it even exists? What role does this spiritual DNA play in our lives? Most importantly, can we alter our spiritual DNA?

A KABBALIST, A GENETICIST

Perhaps the very first geneticist was Abraham the Patriarch, who lived about 4,000 years ago. The founder of three great religions—Judaism, Islam, and Christianity—Abraham also composed the *Sefer Yetzirah*, or *Book of Formation*. In this book, Abraham presented the blueprint of kabbalistic wisdom—a metaphysical structure known as the *Ten Sfirot*, or Ten Luminous Emanations. Using this system, Abraham was able to describe the workings of our solar system and our galaxy as we know them today. Abraham also knew that there were DNA-like forces permeating all reality at every level, and that these forces, when combined in various ways, were responsible for the creation of the people on earth, the planets that occupy our solar system, and the particles that reside in the subatomic world.

According to Abraham, the spiritual DNA in our souls is transferred to each of us through a very precise and complex mechanism: the planets of our solar system. These planets are the devices whereby an individual's spiritual DNA is imprinted into the soul. The nature of the imprint is determined by the exact time of birth and the corresponding arrangement of planets and stars. These ancient teachings are the root and precursor of the science of astrology. But make no mistake, **conventional pop astrology and the kabbalistic system for studying star formation and planetary conditions are as different from each other as night and day.**

THE FOLLY OF POP ASTROLOGY

I f you've heard the question once, you've heard it a thousand and one times: *What's your sign?* And if you're like most people, you've probably had no trouble answering it. You could probably even offer a pretty accurate description of the characteristics of your astrological sign. The fact is, almost everyone knows something about conventional astrology, because it's everywhere; it's a part of popular culture.

Suppose, for example, you wanted to find out more than what's supplied to you by your newspaper's daily astrology column. All you'd have to do is step into any bookstore or library, and the shelves would be overflowing with information on conventional astrology. You could even go online to a thousand different astrology sites. The point is, if you're looking to learn more about conventional astrology, you won't have to go very far; it's there for the taking.

Unfortunately, however, conventional astrology provides as much real insight into your destiny as a Chinese fortune cookie. In this book, we'll explore a very different and far more powerful approach. Quite simply, Kabbalah offers the oldest and wisest application of astronomy and astrology known to humankind. As practiced by the kabbalist, the probing of planets and the study of stars is a true science through which we can understand and satisfy our own deepest needs as well as those of others.

Unlike conventional astrology, which insists that everything we do is determined by the heavens, the kabbalistic study of planets and star formation tells us that we are each born at the precise instant that is best suited to our special needs so that we can exercise our free will. Kabbalah teaches that we have many possible futures, and that through kabbalistic wisdom we can become captains of our own ship and masters of our own destiny.

In the chapters that follow, you'll learn much more of what this means. We'll introduce you to a few definitions of Kabbalah, and just a little history.

We'll present basic kabbalistic precepts in an easily understandable form, and we'll see how these basic ideas have been applied to the planets of our solar system and to the stars that lie beyond.

We'll show you how to begin using the tools of Kabbalah to gain control over your life, to understand and overcome any obstacles in your path, and to increase your well-being both spiritually and materially.

So . . . let's get started.

ORIGINS OF KABBALAH

L ong before the invention of the telescope, Abraham
the Patriarch knew that there were ten planets in our
region of space—the sun, the moon, Mercury, Mars,
Venus, Jupiter, and Saturn—with the three outer planets,
Neptune, Uranus, and Pluto, wholly invisible to the naked
eye. In fact, the three outer planets would not be detected for
several thousand years to come. Abraham also knew how
many years it took the most distant planet, Pluto, to revolve
around the sun—248 years—even though this planet would
not be discovered for yet another four millennia. Abraham
recorded this knowledge in his *Book of Formation*, which carried the seed of all subsequent astronomical knowledge and
kabbalistic wisdom.

The most comprehensive work of Kabbalah is *The Zohar*, or
Book of Splendor, written by Rabbi Shimon Bar Yochai around
200 C.E. Building on the *Book of Formation*, *The Zohar*
encompasses extensive commentary and vast spiritual
insight—as well as key ideas about planetary influences and
how they affect our lives.

The *Book of Formation* and *The Zohar* are the bedrock of kabbalistic knowledge—and nothing in either book is in opposition to the findings of modern science. Both spiritual and scientific disciplines seek to uncover basic truths about the world and our place in it. Scientific disciplines such as physics, astronomy, and medicine examine the world we can see, hear, and touch. Spiritual disciplines such as meditation and astrology study the world that lies beyond the physical realm.

But reality, both spiritual and scientific, turns out to be a pretty slippery thing. We all think we know what it is, but the closer we look the less clear it becomes. In the last hundred years, science has discovered that *how* we look at something may be more important than *what* we look at—and that our expectations may be the most important factor determining what we see.

Kabbalah considers the spiritual and the physical worlds to be equally worthy of investigation and analysis. Kabbalah recognizes that these two worlds are not isolated from each other, and that there are necessary and solid links between them.

Kabbalah identifies the link between the spiritual and the physical worlds—the Upper World and the World Below—as the *Desire to Receive*, and humankind is the highest embodiment of that desire. In other words, **humanity is a bridge between the spiritual and the physical realms.**

AS ABOVE, SO BELOW

K abbalah teaches that there are four levels or dimensions of reality: Emanation (*Atzilut*), Creation (*Briyah*), Formation (*Yetzirah*), and Action (*Asiyah*). For now, it's enough to know that the first dimension, Emanation, is the highest level, and the fourth dimension, Action, is the lowest. But Action is very important to us, because "we live in a material world." Cars, the moon, trees, rocks, your children—they're all here in the realm of Action. Yet all four dimensions are formed in the same way. Everything that happens in the first dimension is repeated in the one below, and so on from top to bottom.

All four levels, then, contain the same essence. The only difference between the higher levels and those below is the quality of the essence. In the highest dimension, the essence is absolutely pure. As it filters down through the different levels, its purity diminishes bit by bit until it reaches our physical world. This filtering process is actually a good thing, as it prevents us from receiving more Light than we can handle.

This process might be compared to a rubber stamp and the image it produces. When we press the stamp onto a piece of paper, every detail engraved on the stamp is reproduced and now visible on the piece of paper. But each time we use the stamp, the image gets a little harder to see—the forms are all there, but the image is slightly less clear than before. In much the same way, each dimension represents the stamped image of the dimension just above it—only the quality of the form is a little less distinct. All the things and happenings in one dimension are copied in the one below. Everything found in this world must have its counterpart in the worlds above.

Kabbalists have a phrase to describe this process: *As above, so below*. Our world is the seeable, touchable, hearable, smellable, and tastable form of all the hidden spiritual worlds. There is nothing in our physical world that does not come from the worlds above. **Kabbalah tells us that everything we see in this world is only a reflection, an approximation, a clue, to something beyond outward appearances.**

Take a minute to think about this. Perhaps you should put this book down, walk outside, and take a close look at the trees, the birds, and people passing on the street. Every one of these things is, first and foremost, a seeable reflection of a hidden spiritual essence that reaches all the way up into the highest levels of the universe.

The Zohar puts it this way:

"You who do not know, but who nonetheless aspire to understand, ponder over what is revealed and manifested [in the
world], and you will understand all that is concealed . . .
because everything to which the Creator has given corporeal
form has been created in the image of that which is above."

A very, very long time ago—science says at least 15 billion
years ago—our universe exploded into existence with the Big
Bang. If it weren't for the Big Bang, we wouldn't be here, nor
would the planets, the stars, or anything else. The Big Bang
is when time began. That's what science says, and Kabbalah
agrees. Kabbalah tells us that before the Big Bang there was
an infinite force of positive energy. It had no beginning and
no end. In Aramaic, the word used to describe this energy
force is called *Or*, which means Light. Before the Big Bang,
there was nothing but Light. There was no space, there was
no time, there was no motion. Kabbalah refers to the Light
as the first cause. There are no other causes before it.

ACRUX

BETA CRUCIS

AGENA

RIGIL K

SPICA

ANTARES

AON 05

Section II:

THE MOMENT
"BEFORE" CREATION

DEFINING LIGHT

The Light is everything positive.

To make this concept easier to comprehend, take a few minutes to make a list of the best moments of your life—that unbelievable catch you made in a baseball game when you were nine, the day you were able to buy your first car, the night the one you loved said they loved you too, the moment your first child was born. It doesn't have to be a long list, but all of us have had at least a few moments when we were filled with a sense of happiness and hope, and the world seemed like it was made just for us.

Now mix all these moments together, magnify them by a factor of about 15 billion, and understand that it's still not even a microscopic speck compared to the never-ending feeling of peace, fulfillment, and pleasure that is the essence of the Light. The moments that made your list—the feelings of accomplishment, faith, and contentment that you experienced—are all manifestations of a portion of the Light. The Light is the bond that holds a marriage together, the force that heals a broken arm or a wounded heart, the power that creates faith in the future. All this and more is included within the Light.

If the whole nature of the Light is to give—the *Desire to Share*—and all there was in the beginning was the Light, what was there to give to?

The Light wanted to share, yet it had nothing to share with. Obviously, something had to be done. So the Light created a Vessel to receive everything it had to offer. Receiving was the Vessel's whole job, its only job—the *Desire to Receive*. Kabbalah teaches that the Light is the first cause, and the Vessel the first effect.

According to Kabbalah, the creation of the Vessel, with its *Desire to Receive*, is the only creation that ever took place. Everything else was a result of that creation.

So we had the Light, whose whole nature was to give of itself. We had the Vessel, whose whole nature was to receive all the positive things that the Light had to share. The Vessel was filling up with the Light, and because time and space hadn't even begun yet, the Vessel was filling endlessly. The Vessel kept receiving, and the Light kept giving. It was perfect; it was paradise.

But then a strange thing happened.

The Vessel inherited from its Creator the traits of sharing and desiring to be the cause.

This *Desire to Share* felt very good to the Vessel. In fact, the Vessel wanted to start doing some sharing of its own, to shed some Light of its own. It wanted to become more of a cause and less of an effect.

But how could the Vessel express the *Desire to Share* if its very nature was to receive? How could the Vessel be the cause of its own fulfillment if it was merely the effect? Sharing, after all, wasn't part of its job. So the Vessel made a decision. The Vessel pushed back the Light and said, "No more!"

The moment the Vessel pushed back the Light and stopped being simply an effect, the Light said, "Okay, I understand your need to evolve and express yourself." Just as a loving parent who stands back to allow a toddler to take his or her first tentative steps, the Light withdrew. It gave the Vessel the space to learn about sharing and the opportunity to become a causative force in the process of creation. The Vessel now had a space in which it could express its own sharing nature. This space was the cause of the creation of our physical realm.

The ancient kabbalists called the Vessel's act of pushing back the Light "Restriction." Science calls it . . . THE BIG BANG.

THE BIG BANG

A ccording to Kabbalah, once the *Restriction* took place, the Vessel exploded into zillions and zillions of pieces. The pieces of the shattered Vessel became all the fragments of matter and energy that make up our entire universe—atoms, animals, people, planets, everything. In this way, the Vessel could share with itself and with the Light, thereby becoming the cause of its own fulfillment.

Everything in the universe is a portion of the original Vessel. Kabbalistically, the *Desire to Receive* is the secret engine that drives everything in the universe and is, in fact, indispensable to the world's functioning.

In order to look more closely at this idea, let's review what we've learned so far:

- There is nothing in our physical world that does not originate in the spiritual worlds above.

- Before time began, all that existed was an infinite force of positive energy that Kabbalah calls the Light.

- The Light's main characteristic is its *Desire to Share* all the beneficence that it contains.

- In order to share, the Light created the Vessel.

- The Vessel was made by the Light. Its main characteristic was the *Desire to Receive* all that the Light had to offer.

- One of the qualities the Vessel received from the Light was the *Desire to Share*—the desire to be the cause of its own pleasure. But the Vessel couldn't share or be the cause while it was in a constant state of receiving.

- So the Vessel pushed back the Light. Separating from the Light for the first time, the Vessel exploded into all the fragments of matter and energy that make up our universe. And since the Vessel's main characteristic was the *Desire to Receive*, all the fragments that make up our universe contain aspects of this desire.

Even rocks and stones have a little bit of the *Desire to Receive*. As we move up the scale of Creation, we see an increasing physical dependence on the external world—a carrot needs more from the world than a rock, and a cow needs more than a carrot. But human beings have by far the greatest *Desire to*

Receive, because we not only need material things such as water, air, and food, we also require intangibles such as peace, hope, love, and fulfillment.

Remember, according to the wisdom of Kabbalah: " . . . the unifying link between the spiritual and the physical worlds— the Upper World and the World Below—is the *Desire to Receive* the Light of the Creator . . . and humanity is the highest embodiment of that desire."

In other words, Kabbalah tells us that *people* are the missing link between the spiritual and physical worlds.

How does that work, exactly? How are we the unifying link between our world and the worlds above?

To answer this question, let's revisit our list, and everywhere it says "the Vessel," put in the word "humanity." When you're finished, the list should look something like this:

- There is nothing in our physical world that does not originate in the spiritual worlds above.

- Before time began, all that existed was an infinite force of positive energy that Kabbalah calls the Light.

- The Light's main characteristic was its *Desire to Share* all the beneficence that it contains. In order to share, the Light created humanity.

- Humanity was made by the Light. Its main characteristic was its *Desire to Receive* all that the Light had to offer.

- One of the qualities that humanity received from the Light was the *Desire to Share* and to be the cause of its own pleasure. But it couldn't share while it was in a constant state of receiving.

- Humanity pushed back the Light.

Humanity became the Vessel to receive the blessings of the Light.

We are made up of two essential elements: our body or our ego, the Vessel whose true nature begins and ends with the *Desire to Receive for the Self Alone*—and our soul, which embodies the *Desire to Receive for the Sake of Sharing*.

DESIRE TO RECEIVE

The ultimate transformation of the human *Desire to Receive* is found in the *Desire to Receive for the Sake of Sharing*. Remember, this *Desire to Share* was the reason that the Vessel chose to push the Light away. **It is when the *Desire to Receive* is transformed into the *Desire to Receive for the Sake of Sharing* that we are most like the Light and become the cause of our own fulfillment.** According to Kabbalah, we actually reunite with the Light at the moment we emulate its sharing nature. In this way, we serve as the link between the physical world and the spiritual world above. By exercising our potential for sharing, we form a connection to the Light that created us. And, as with any good exercise that makes us stronger, the more we share, the greater our potential becomes.

From a kabbalistic perspective, sharing is receiving. When we share, we might have the impression that we are giving something up, but in fact we create a flow of energy from the spiritual world that replaces our loss. This does not mean that if we give someone a dollar, we'll find a dollar in our pockets when we get home—that dollar's gone, make no mistake about it. But our capacity to receive the Light increases with every act of sharing we commit. So an apparent loss at the physical level is balanced out by an increase of Light on the spiritual level.

The result of our sharing might be a positive effect on our health or in our relationships, or we might receive something too subtle and mysterious to notice right away. But whether we notice it or not, we can be certain that for every act of sharing, a deposit is made into our spiritual bank accounts.

The only purpose of the *Desire to Receive* is to attract the infinite blessings of the Light. This is the whole reason for our existence in the physical world.

But what about those people who receive money, power, and happiness without even thinking about sharing? Kabbalah recognizes that we can, at any time we wish, selfishly receive the blessings of the Light. Very often, our *Desire to Receive* degenerates into a self-centered *Desire to Receive for the Self Alone.* It forgets its true purpose and it is led astray by the pleasures of this earthly existence.

But physical or spiritual satisfaction will not endure unless there is balance between receiving and sharing. For example, we might achieve success in business by exerting our *Desire to Receive for the Self Alone*, but there will eventually be darkness and chaos in another area of our lives—in our health, in our relationships, or in our emotional well-being. So why settle for less? We can have it all if we just learn how to "receive" from the Light in a balanced way.

Giving and receiving—becoming a cause rather than an effect—is the goal of our existence. We cannot continue to receive the Light unless we share the Light. If we are only receivers, we become merely reactive to the events and circumstances around us. Put another way, the more we give from the Vessel, the more room we have for what we will receive in turn. Consider an eight-ounce glass: The glass can hold only eight ounces of water, and that's it. But cut a tiny hole in the bottom of the glass and allow the water to fill other cups, and suddenly water can flow endlessly.

This idea of a voluntary *Desire to Receive for the Sake of Sharing* is one of the most insightful truths that Kabbalah has to offer. We stress the word "voluntary" because choice is at the root of Kabbalah's insight. Kabbalah recognizes that the Vessel itself, and not the Light, made its own choice. It exercised free will. It was no longer just a receiver. By choosing to restrict the Light until it could share, the Vessel went from being simply the first effect to being the first effect and a cause in its own right. It became proactive—like the Light itself. So the Vessel was the master of its own destiny. **The idea of free will is what makes kabbalistic astrology fundamentally different from conventional pop astrology.**

THE DIFFERENCE BETWEEN
CAUSE AND EFFECT

W hat does it mean to be an effect in this physical world? What does it mean to become the cause? And how does free will fit into this dynamic?

Imagine there's a sudden downturn in your business. You become upset, worried, or frightened. Suppose a friend insults you and you feel hurt, angry, and even vengeful.

In both situations, an external event was the cause of your inner feelings. You merely reacted to a situation. Your feelings were the effect of something outside yourself.

But what if things take a turn for the better?

Business improves. You're ecstatic, brimming with confidence. Then someone you admire pays you a compliment. You're flattered and gratified. Once again, something external is the cause of your emotions. Again, you are merely reacting to a situation outside yourself. The situation was the cause, and your good feelings were the effect.

In contrast, let's examine what it means to be the cause.

A financial crisis strikes. You're about to panic. But you remember that your purpose in life is to become the cause, not just the effect. Instead of reacting in a panic, you let go. You focus your attention on your response. You realize that you have the power to determine your own happiness—that it is not dependent on the ups and downs of a business cycle.

Then, suddenly, business is booming again. Instead of reacting with happiness and joy at the prospect of higher profits, you acknowledge that your happiness should be present regardless of outside forces. This simple acknowledgement puts you in control of your inner life. **You are the cause of your feelings.**

When we receive the Light directly, as we did when we were first created, we are merely an effect. However, when the Light is concealed, and we have to earn it by resisting our reactive instincts, the Light is then revealed. We are the cause of its revelation.

Imagine a kind, old puzzle maker whose greatest joy is creating the most delightful pictures for children and turning them into puzzles. The puzzle maker is responsible for creating the original picture. His goal is to bestow pleasure by creating the most enchanting pictures. But no child wants to receive a puzzle that is already fully assembled, no matter how enchanting or amazing the completed picture is. The real joy is in assembling the puzzle. When a child rebuilds the puzzle and gazes at the completed image, he or she feels a sense of ownership and accomplishment. The child becomes the cause behind the creation of the image.

In assembling a puzzle, we may put pieces in the wrong places. But that challenge gives value and meaning to the right moves when we do finally make them.

That's life! The Light disassembled the puzzle of Creation at the behest of the Vessel so that we could rebuild it, spiritually speaking. And yes, we tend to make both wrong and right moves in this puzzle of life. But each time we stop reacting to external events and resist our natural self-seeking tendencies, we connect another piece of the puzzle. Each time we restrict the urge to react and instead are proactive, another piece is put in place.

People often discredit astrology when two individuals, born at the exact same time in the same place, lead completely different lives. The positions of their planets are identical, right? Why don't their lives follow exactly the same paths?

Kabbalah would answer this way: It's because your life is not determined by the positions of the planets!

"What?!?" you may say. "Run that by me again."

Your life is not determined by the positions of the planets.
In fact, it would be more correct to say that the positions of
the planets are determined by your life, or lives.

Your birth occurred at a particular moment because it was at
that precise moment that your soul needed to be born. In
other words, it wasn't by chance that you were born at exactly
8:43 P.M. on July 21, 1958, in Chicago, Illinois. Chance had
nothing to do with it. As Albert Einstein said, "God does not
play dice with the universe." And neither do our souls play
games with us.

Each of us was born at the precise moment that gave us the
best opportunity to become more like the Light and ascend to
a higher level of consciousness. Put another way, we're here
to get better at sharing and to become the cause of our own
fulfillment—and, in so doing, we reconnect to the Light that
made us.

Kabbalah tells us that our present life is an aggregate of all
our previous lives. In our previous lives, we faced problems
and challenges and made certain choices. Some of these
choices were good ones—they resulted in the growth of our
Desire to Receive for the Sake of Sharing and the evolution of
our souls. Some of those choices meant that we were *NOT*
just reacting to outside forces. Instead, we resisted and
became the cause of our own feelings. But some of our choices weren't so good—they resulted in the growth of our *Desire
to Receive for the Self Alone*, and they limited the growth of our
souls. We reacted to the outside influences that life threw at

us. We succumbed to all the temptations that gratified our egos without any regard to the person next to us.

Through the process of reincarnation, we return to an astrological location that gives us the best opportunity possible to revisit those not-so-good choices. This time, we can make different choices and overcome the limitations that held back the growth of our souls. We must play the game until we get it right. It's just like kids playing a video game—they keep playing and losing and learning and remembering, until they figure out all the tricks of the game, work their way through all the levels, and . . . they win!

Except that the game of life is a little harder. In the game of life, each time we play, we seem to forget that we ever played before. It always seems like the first time.

Most of us can't remember how we lived those past lives, or where we failed, or what choices limited the growth of our *Desire to Receive for the Sake of Sharing*.

So when those same choices rise up before us again in this life, how can we make better decisions?

To begin to answer this question, imagine you're on a cosmic road trip. Your journey is influenced by all the other road trips you've ever taken, but you can't remember any of them. The route is littered with all kinds of detours and patches of unpaved road and places you might avoid if only you could remember what you did on your last trip. But since you can't remember, you get all turned around. You get lost and never quite reach your destination, so you feel frustrated and unfulfilled, disappointed and unhappy.

Sound familiar? Wouldn't it be nice if someone could hand us a map when we start out, to help us navigate our way around all the trouble spots?

Well, there is such a map.

The map clearly identifies the kinds of choices we've made before and suggests alternate routes for reaching the best destination we can hope to attain on this particular trip.

And Kabbalah tells us it's all right there in the genetic code of our souls, otherwise known as our astrological chart.

ACRUX

BETA CRUCIS

AGENA

RIGIL K

SPICA

ANTARES

Section III:

SPIRITUAL
EVOLUTION

FREE WILL

Conventional astrology says that our characters are determined by the position of the planets or stars. All the decisions have already been made. It's over; we're stuck with it; it's out of our hands.

The sages of Kabbalah tell us that we're born at the precise moment that gives us the best chance at being the best we can be. Kabbalah says that we're going to have choices in this life just as we have had choices in our past lives. Our past choices have determined where we start out, and our present choices will determine where we end up. The decisions are ours to make. Our fate is in our own hands.

We've had free will right from the beginning of time. It was the Vessel that chose to push away the Light in order to realize its potential for sharing and become the cause of its own destiny. The Vessel said, "No more Light unless I can become a causative force." If it weren't for that first act of free will, we wouldn't be here today—no Restriction, no Big Bang, no universe as we know it. Ever since, we've been making both good and bad decisions, but we've been making them ourselves. It is precisely on this issue of free will that Kabbalah differs from conventional astrology.

But with free will comes responsibility. We are responsible for where we find ourselves. We are driving our own cars.

That means we can't blame our mothers, our fathers, our bosses, or even the Creator for the position we may find ourselves in. Some of our choices in previous lives weren't so good as far as the growth of our souls was concerned. Some were self-serving and did nothing to improve our ability to share and become more like the Light. Indeed, we might have let all kinds of external episodes and material possessions control and motivate our entire existence. We were merely the effect, tossed about like a ping-pong ball by peer pressure, jealousy, and blind ambition. In fact, those self-serving choices we made in previous lives have set up obstacles that we are now being asked to overcome in this life.

These obstacles are actually good things, though, for they are what makes life interesting and challenging. What, after all, is a high-hurdles race without the hurdles?

But here's the most important thing: What we have built, we can tear down.

Conventional astrology says, "You are imprisoned by the positions of the planets and stars." Kabbalah says, "If you want to call it a prison, it is a prison of your own making. Your past choices have built the walls. Your present choices can tear those walls down."

One of the most powerful tools for pulling down those walls is called *tikkun*, which is Aramaic for "correction."

The kabbalistic concept of *tikkun* reveals the kinds of choices we've made in past lives and, more important, which choices we should make this time around.

By understanding our personal *tikkun* we can:

- Identify our past weaknesses.

- Recognize the baggage we've brought along from previous lives.

- Avoid the roadblocks and detours that slow our progress toward the Light.

- Overcome our deepest fears.

- Become "all that we can be" in the deepest sense.

Think of a big interstellar space ship on its way to a distant star. On board is a computer that keeps the rocket on course. Along its route, the rocket passes strange planets and stars that exert gravitational pull on its hull, but the computer keeps the flight path straight and true, making corrections whenever needed.

We are that rocket. The physical universe is the computer, the planets and stars the hardware, and *tikkun* is the software that keeps our individual lives on course.

Without *tikkun*, the rocket is certain to be pulled off course by various influences. In other words, without taking into account our "point of correction," we are doomed to be pushed and pulled through life by the positions of our stars. Our *tikkun* shows us the way, shows us the work we need to do on ourselves. It is up to us to make the corrections that keep the rocket on course.

On an astrological chart, the *tikkun* is called the lunar node. Lunar, of course, refers to the moon, which is very important in Kabbalah because it represents the *Desire to Receive*.

The lunar node is made up of two diametrically opposed poles: the south node and the north node.

The south node describes all the baggage that we've brought along from previous lives.

The north node describes the path or the correction to take in our present life.

Together, they are the keys to self-realization.

Every good sailor knows that the position of the stars reveals where we are. More importantly, Kabbalah teaches that the stars can also show where we came from and how to get where we're going.

THE REASON FOR DNA IN
OUR SOULS

The DNA in our soul sets us on a course of life that will help transform our *Desire to Receive* to a *Desire to Receive for the Sake of Sharing*—or, put another way, to become more like the Light that made us.

To help us accomplish this, Abraham the Patriarch and other great kabbalists revealed information about the influence that the stars and planets exert each month. With this basic information, we can spot various energies that work on us every moment of our lives. We can then make use of the helpful energies while protecting ourselves from the harmful ones.

There are no bad signs or bad moments, only different opportunities. Understanding these opportunities makes it easier for us to make our corrections and do the work that's needed to lift our souls. Kabbalah has a special way of seeing the world that makes us the link between the Upper World and the World Below. Remember, humanity was created as the Vessel to receive the Light.

But the Light is powerful. If we were to receive it all at once, it would be like getting hit by a bolt of lightning—too much power, too fast.

Kabbalah tells us that the stars and the planets are like filters that enable us to receive the Light safely. Each astrological configuration, each month and its corresponding sign, blocks out most of the Light but allows a manageable portion to reach us in the physical world. The characteristics of the portion of the Light that we receive are different for every month/sign. That's why each month/sign has its own unique strengths and weaknesses.

As you've probably already guessed, the month/sign when we were born has the strongest influence on our journey through life. This is because it is at the moment of birth that the soul enters the physical body.

With our very first breath, we receive the seed of our whole life.

But doesn't that mean our whole existence is predetermined? If the seed of our life is all there in our first breath, why not just lie there like a fish and let "whatever" happen to us?

Kabbalah would answer, "Because a seed is just a seed. It's a possible tree. It is up to us to choose from all the different possible paths presented to us by that first breath."

Given the right care, the right food, the right Light, the seed grows into the best tree it can be. But if we don't do the necessary

work on ourselves—if we don't consciously seek to transform
our *Desire to Receive* into a *Desire to Receive for the Sake of
Sharing*, if we don't use our *tikkun* to keep ourselves on
course—we will remain at the mercy of the planets. The positions of the planets at the moment of our birth do not determine our whole life; they merely influence it. They are the
seeds, not the whole tree.

And that's not all. Beyond the influence of our birth sign,
Kabbalah tells us that we are also influenced by the energies
of the planets at every moment. So it isn't enough just to
know the strengths and weaknesses of our birth signs; it is
also important to understand each month's/sign's strengths
and weaknesses. Understanding the characteristics and energies of each month/sign allows us to plan our actions with
confidence and certainty, regardless of when we were born.

Kabbalah tells us that we live within a predictable cycle of
influences that return every year. Once we are familiar with
this cycle, we can use the positive influences for our benefit
and for our protection from negative influences. This simple
truth is one of Kabbalah's greatest contributions to practical
human wisdom: the ability to schedule actions at their most
advantageous times.

A few years ago, NASA sent a probe to explore the outer
planets of our solar system. In order to get the rocket to its
destination, the scientists timed the launch so that the probe
could use Jupiter's gravity as a slingshot toward Neptune. In
other words, by understanding the physical nature of Jupiter's

influence on the probe, the scientists were able to use Jupiter for their own purpose.

In the same way, Kabbalah allows us to use our understanding of the spiritual influence of the planets and stars for our own spiritual purpose. By making the necessary corrections to our life path, we can give ourselves the best chance of spiritual success.

Kabbalah's understanding of these spiritual influences is very precise. Every lunar month is divided into three periods, each with its own particular energy. According to kabbalistic teaching, the first ten days of a lunar month are generally positive and are therefore a good time to take action. The first day of a lunar month is particularly positive, offering an opportunity to connect to the full potential of energy waiting to be manifested throughout the whole month.

The middle ten days of the month are divided into five positive and five negative days. The first five are positive until the full moon, which in the lunar calendar always falls on the 15th day. After the full moon, the positive energy of the month becomes very difficult to reveal; hence the five negative days, whose energy continues through into the final ten or so days remaining in the month. All things being equal, for example, Kabbalah tells us that a person planning to start a new business will be better off signing the papers in the early part of the lunar month rather than at the end of the month.

In this way and in many others, Kabbalah provides a way of knowing the different possibilities and opportunities that are built into every day and every instant of time. How we use these possibilities and take advantage of the opportunities is up to us.

THE CALENDAR

Y ou know what day it is, don't you? If you happen to forget for a moment, you can probably check that calendar hanging on the wall of your kitchen, or perhaps the one sitting on your desk in the office, or the one on your computer or cell phone. In fact, the calendar is so much a part of our lives that we almost don't notice it anymore. The days of the week are just there, like the air we breathe.

But unlike the air, calendars are created by people to divide time into usable fragments. Without calendars, the days, months, and years would blend together into an undifferentiated, monotonous mess—we'd be looking for the Sunday paper on Tuesday. In fact, so profound is this influence on our lives that the various calendar systems separate the cultures that use them as distinctly as they separate days, weeks, and months.

The Western world's Gregorian calendar is based on the earth's orbit around the sun. It is composed of approximately

365 days in a regular year and 366 days in each leap year (every fourth year). With the solar calendar, the position of the sun in conjunction with the seasons is always the same. March 21st is always the beginning of the northern spring. If you live in the United States, this is probably the calendar that is attached to your refrigerator.

Another system, the Muslim calendar, is based on the orbit of the moon around the earth. It is made up of 12 months of 29 or 30 days each. The Muslim lunar year, or the passing of 12 new moons, comes to approximately 354 days, which makes the Muslim year about 11 days shorter than the solar or Gregorian year. Because of this difference between the lunar and solar years, any given month in the Muslim calendar may fall during any of the solar seasons. As a result, Muslim holidays don't necessarily occur during the same season.

The kabbalistic calendar is based on the lunar year of 12 months with 29 or 30 days each, with each month corresponding to one of the 12 signs of the zodiac. But because all cosmic holidays and festivals, such as *Rosh Hashanah* and Passover, occur on days mandated by The Bible according to the lunar month within a particular season of the solar year, the lunar year must be reconciled with the solar year to prevent holidays from wandering through the seasons as in the Muslim calendar. To accomplish this goal, seven times in every 19 years the kabbalistic calendar has a leap year with an additional 13th month, *Adar II*—a second month of Pisces. This maintains an approximate correspondence between the kabbalistic/lunar calendar and the Gregorian/solar calendar.

At the same time, a person's birth sign may be different on the kabbalistic calendar than it is on the Gregorian calendar.

If you would like to know your lunar birth date and discover if your lunar astrological sign differs from your conventional sign, please contact one of our instructors at student support at 1-800-KABBALAH.

ARAMAIC SIGNS IN THE HEAVENS

Accoding to Kabbalah, the 22 Aramaic letters are the building blocks of the entire universe, with each letter revealing an aspect of Creation. The Aramaic letters are the genetic alphabet of the entire universe. This is not just a metaphor. Although it is beyond the scope of this book, Kabbalah teaches that the letters of the Aramaic alphabet are the actual stuff of which the universe is made. Each letter has a very specific and powerful spiritual energy.

Twelve letters are the actual DNA code for the 12 signs of the zodiac.

Hei is the DNA code that created Aries

Vav is the DNA code that created Taurus

Zayin is the DNA code that created Gemini

Chet is the DNA code that created Cancer

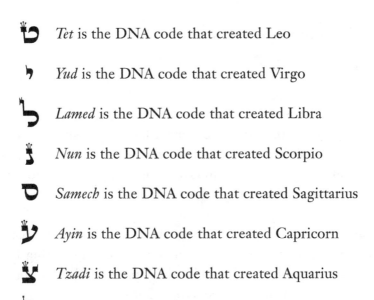

Tet is the DNA code that created Leo

Yud is the DNA code that created Virgo

Lamed is the DNA code that created Libra

Nun is the DNA code that created Scorpio

Samech is the DNA code that created Sagittarius

Ayin is the DNA code that created Capricorn

Tzadi is the DNA code that created Aquarius

Kuf is the DNA code that created Pisces

The remaining seven letters are the DNA forces that created the sun, the moon, and the first five planets.

Chaf created the Sun

Tav created the Moon

Reish created Mercury

Pei created Venus

Dalet created Mars

Gimel created Jupiter

 Bet created Saturn

From this we see that there are two Aramaic letters associated with every month—one letter for the heavenly body that rules the month, and another letter for the corresponding sign of the zodiac. These two letters enable us to connect to the inner spiritual energy of each month.

The letters are the keys or the "passwords" that give us access to a particular month's source of spiritual energy. Using the Aramaic letters helps us reunite the Upper World, the spiritual world, with the physical World Below.

ACRUX

BETA CRUCI

AGENA

RIGIL K

SPICA

ANTARES

30 NOV 6

CRACKING THE CODE
OF THE SOUL

The Torah speaks in detail about the 12 tribes of Israel, and goes to great lengths to define the positions of the 12 tribes and their encampments in the desert—three tribes on the east side, three tribes on the south, and so on.

According to Kabbalah, these passages metaphorically refer to the 12 constellations and their positions in the heavens. And these 12 signs give us insights into our spiritual genetic makeup.

This section discusses each sign and constellation in the night sky and its corresponding lunar month. We provide a description of the month's/sign's spiritual DNA and the characteristics and energies associated with it, and we suggest ways to express the strengths and control the weaknesses inherent in them.

These descriptions don't pretend to be exhaustive or complete. They are merely introductions to a much larger body of knowledge, which we hope will encourage you to dig deeper. If you look carefully at the characteristics of any of the signs, you'll notice that each characteristic is a sort of double-edged sword. For example, single-mindedness by itself can be a very positive feature, expressing itself as consistency, stability, or persistence in the face of hardship. But a selfish single-mindedness can quickly become childish stubbornness. In the same way, an intolerance of opposition at the service of a good cause is a positive quality—but when selfishly applied, it soon becomes narrow-mindedness and fanaticism.

It is not the sword itself, but how you choose to wield the sword that counts. Kabbalah recognizes that the influence of your birth month/sign can take you in many directions, and it is up to you to choose the path. The goal of Kabbalah is to help lift the level of your soul, to transform your *Desire to Receive* to a *Desire to Receive for the Sake of Sharing*—to become more like the Light that made you.

If the following descriptions seem to sound negative to you, remember that **obstacles provide us with the opportunity to choose differently this time around.** It's only when we face these challenges that we can overcome our fears and move forward toward the Light.

Read all the months/signs, not just your birth month. Each month is pertinent because we all have to find our way through the entire year. Each month suggests its own possibilities and opportunities for improving our lives.

To determine the sign which represents your *tikkun*—point of correction—please refer to the *tikkun* reference table on page 188.

THE MONTH OF *NISSAN* (ARIES)

Rebels without a Cause

*N*issan is the first month of the lunar year. It always coincides with the northern spring (around late March on the Gregorian calendar). Ruled by the planet Mars and named after the Roman god of war, it is a month filled with opportunities in the form of confrontations, battles, and potential antagonism. Because of this, Kabbalah tells us that the force of miracles is present in the universe during the month of *Nissan*.

The Aramaic letters connecting us to the positive aspects of the month are *Hei* ה, which created the sign of Aries and represents the *Desire to Receive*, and *Dalet* ד, which created Mars and means "poor." The combination of these two letters is interpreted to mean that during the month of *Nissan*, we should strive to diminish our *Desire to Receive for the Self Alone*. By contemplating these two Aramaic letters, we can tap into the energy necessary to attain this goal.

The strengths and weaknesses of those born under the influence of Aries are linked with the ideas of seeds, infancy, or immaturity—a unique potential for growth coupled with a tendency toward impulsiveness and stubbornness; a pioneering spirit, boundless enthusiasm, courage, and a love of freedom combined with a total disregard for the consequences of one's actions. Like very young children, Aries tend to think of themselves as the center of the universe, and when they want something, they want it now.

According to the *Book of Formation* (*Sefer Yetzirah*), each sign of the zodiac corresponds to a different part of the body. Aries is associated with the head. Like the Ram that represents this sign, Aries rushes into things head first. If Aries is suddenly taken with an idea at four o'clock in the morning, they take action immediately. If someone should question their decisions, they become indignant. When Aries believes in something, they dismiss all objections. They cannot tolerate opposition.

Under the influence of Mars, the planet of war, Aries are courageous and even daring. Unafraid of confrontation, they have a tendency to seek it out. Again, like the Ram, Aries have a need to break down all barriers that stand in their way. They hate confinement or limitation of any kind. Danger has no meaning to them. They are quick and direct, but can be burdened by inflexibility and a lack of diplomacy. As a fire sign, their tempers tend to flare easily.

If this sounds a lot like some teenagers you know, it isn't by accident. In many ways, Aries are "rebels without a cause."

If you look carefully at the characteristics of Aries, their dou-ble-edged sword is, in fact, exactly what was described in the previous chapter: single-mindedness expressing itself on the one hand as consistency, stability, or persistence in the face of hardship, and on the other hand as *childlike stubbornness*.

So for Aries in particular, this means their *tikkun* is all about putting themselves at the service of a cause that goes beyond *Desire to Receive for the Self Alone*. It means transforming the love of freedom for its own sake to the love of a higher free-dom that liberates them from the grip of selfish impulses. True freedom is not about a petulant "I can do anything I want;" it's about mastering the ego. Impetuous action does not necessarily make an Aries free. On the contrary, it may enslave them to momentary impulse and empty whim.

Aries need to put themselves at the service of a cause that goes beyond the *Desire to Receive for the Self Alone*. It means trans-forming love of freedom for its own sake into love of a high-er freedom that liberates from the grip of selfish impulses.

In fact, because Aries' *Desire to Receive* is so strong, they have the greatest potential for transforming their *Desire to Receive* into a *Desire to Receive for the Sake of Sharing*. The seed, the potential for transformation, is within them in abundance.

In other words, **by working to correct the self-centered influences of the month/sign, Aries can become positive, proactive channels for the Light and increase their ability**

to receive for the benefit of others. Along this redemptive path, and for the same selfless reasons, they can learn to listen carefully before passing judgment and reflect before taking action. In this way, they can reverse the negative/reactive influences of the sign. This is the battle that Aries were made to fight. In this way, they become *rebels with a cause*.

The word *Nissan* contains the Aramaic word *nes*, which means "miracle." According to Webster, a miracle is ". . . an accomplishment or occurrence so outstanding or unusual as to seem beyond human capability or endeavor . . ." Let's look at what this means for taking advantage of the positive energy that the month has to offer.

The parting of the Red Sea was a miracle. David slaying Goliath was a miracle. Both seemed impossible, beyond human capability. But Kabbalah tells us that miracles happen every second because the Light gives us an opportunity to change our destiny at every point in time.

David was not fighting for himself, but for his people. He was placing himself at the service of an unselfish interest. This was the hard part. This was the miracle. He had already overcome the self-centered aspect of his personality. He had beaten the spiritual giant inside himself before the physical battle ever began. After this, bringing down Goliath was easy.

Specifically, **the month of Nissan allows us to connect to a miraculous energy that helps us overcome and diminish our *Desire to Receive for the Self Alone*.**

IF YOUR *TIKKUN* (CORRECTION) IS IN ARIES . . .

A *tikkun* in Aries tells you that you formerly had the behavior of a Libra (south node). That is, you were often in the role of arbitrator but were unable to settle conflicts because you refused to make decisions. Taking sides was difficult for you, since it implied possibly hurting someone. Because of this, rather than make a clear choice, you tried to unite what was incompatible, and you suffered the consequences of your indecision.

As a Libran, you learned to compromise in order to avoid confrontation. You were overly dependent on the opinion of others, and this often caused you to act aggressively soon after your initial act of submission—classic passive-aggressive behavior!

A *tikkun* in Aries points you toward a correction where you must, above all else, uncover your identity, your unique needs, and your individual desires. You must seek independence and reinforce your self-confidence. This will help you discover your own spiritual nature and enable you to become more proactive in all areas of your life. Along this path of correction, you can stop avoiding confrontations and face each situation as it unfolds, without needing the approval of others.

As you pass each test, you will gain awareness and confidence, come to know your own personality, and strengthen yourself. Combining Libra's altruism with Aries' ability to "fight the good fight" will bring about an overall elevation of your soul, allowing you to become the cause of the fulfillment you will soon receive. And this is what Kabbalah is all about.

THIS MONTH'S INFLUENCE ON ALL OF US:

Confrontation

Aries is ruled by the war planet Mars. War can signify conflict among nations or hostility between two individuals. The spiritual influences arising in this month offer you the emotional strength to triumph over personal conflict and effect reconciliation. *Nissan* is an opportune time to build bridges and make peace with people with whom you're in conflict.

THE MONTH OF *IYAR* (TAURUS)

Bull in the Bubble

*I*yar is the second month of the lunar year, and usually occurs in April or May on the Gregorian calendar. Ruled by the planet Venus, the Roman goddess of love and beauty, *Iyar* is nicknamed the Month of Light.

The Aramaic letters connecting us to *Iyar*'s positive aspects are *Vav* ‫ו‬, which created the sign of Taurus, and *Pei* ‫פ‬, which created the planet Venus. Taken together, these letters tell us that during the month of *Iyar*, the force of judgment is present in the universe.

How are Light and Judgment related? How can we best take advantage of the possibilities this month offers?

As a first step toward understanding the strengths and weaknesses of those born under the influence of Taurus, imagine a bull grazing contentedly in his own little meadow in a sun-drenched valley surrounded by hills. As far as he's concerned, his beautiful little meadow goes on forever. He can't see any fences from where he stands, and he just assumes that there aren't any fences anywhere. Life seems okay where he is, and he imagines it's okay everywhere. Besides, why go looking for trouble? Don't make waves—that's his motto. Live and let live. Things always work out in the end.

So he minds his own business and keeps on grazing, satisfied with the cards he has been dealt. He's loyal, consistent, patient, tolerant, law-abiding, friendly, dependable, non-judgmental—and, heck, he's pretty good-looking to boot. What more could he ask of himself?

Good question. What more *could* he ask of himself?

For most of us, the world is such a patchwork of good and bad, success and failure, darkness and light, beauty and ugliness, that when we see personalities like the Bull's, we are tempted to leave them alone in their comfortable, Pollyannaish bliss. And this is precisely what most Taureans would prefer. They don't want to be changed. They don't want to be bothered. They don't even want to move!

And it's easy to see why. The Light is very warm on their backs.

The world Taureans live in is bathed in Light. Venus, *Nogah* in Aramaic, rules Taurus. *Nogah* means Light. For Taureans, Light is everywhere—a beautiful, dazzling, but sometimes blinding Light. Because of this, Taureans tend to be eternal optimists, focusing on the positive and disregarding the negative.

Nothing seems to upset them. They refuse to attribute bad intentions to anyone. Confronted with a nasty situation, it is not unusual for Taureans to respond with indifference. The situation will right itself—the Light will take care of it. For this reason, Taureans often seem to lack ambition, initiative, and imagination. But it's not that they don't possess these attributes; they just don't see any reason to use them. Because of the abundance of Light in their lives, Taureans can get complacent, self-satisfied, or smug. They are comfortable exactly where they are.

Taureans often look imposing and are usually burly with a wide neck. The organs that correspond to Taurus are the throat and the tonsils, making them prone to sore throats, tonsillitis, or other illnesses specific to this area of the body. Taureans' physical heaviness is generally reflected in their personalities as well; they are docile, placid, and quite stubborn. Their reactions are always measured; they do not panic easily, and they rarely lose their temper. Even their joy is expressed in a restrained manner.

Taureans love comfort. Their houses, spouses, and possessions are all precious to them. Acquiring and keeping these things is one of the ways they express their power. To keep it all intact, they may excuse or ignore any snub, insult, or unpleasantness. Some Taureans will "fiddle while Rome burns" and overlook even the most incontrovertible evidence of impending disaster. They place themselves in a protective bubble of comfort and Light, untouched and unmoved by the negative aspects of the world.

In kabbalistic terms, Taureans may use the Light to deliberately stay in the dark. They are like children hiding under a security blanket where they feel safe, warm, and cozy. When this happens, Taurus's tranquil and unfettered life can be more accurately described as stagnant and cut off from the world. Life in the bubble is safe and comfortable, but it's unconscious in every sense of the word—asleep, unaware, on autopilot.

Fortunately, there is another aspect to this comfortable Light of Venus. Taureans in particular can use this aspect to remain conscious, in touch with the world, vigorous, and full of life. That aspect is judgment. Judgment is the key. Remember: Each astrological configuration, each month of the year, each sign of the zodiac blocks out most of the Light but allows a safe portion of it to get through to us here in the physical world. The characteristics of the portion of the Light that we receive are different for every month/sign.

What characteristics does the Light of Venus allow through? Venus is the only one of the inner planets that rotates in a clockwise direction. According to Kabbalah, any visible expression in the physical world is the result of a spiritual energy in the hidden worlds above us. So the unusual movement of Venus results from a different sort of spiritual energy than all the other planets.

Specifically, Venus moves from left to right because it moves from a spiritual energy of judgment toward a spiritual energy of mercy.

Judgment is the Light's request for revelation. In other words, *Iyar*, the Month of Light, is an opportunity to discover, through use of our judgment, something that was previously unknown to us.

For Taureans in particular, this means that there are choices —judgments—to be made. Although their perception that "things always work out in the end" is true, Taureans must learn that this merciful truth is not revealed fully in our physical world. Mankind must work hard to draw aside the many curtains of darkness and let the Light shine through. To grow, the Bull must leave his bubble and become more proactive, make judgments, and choose good from bad. The very same Light that warms his back gives him the tools to confront the world, not hide from it, and to become more involved in the world, not less.

Any of us can simply accept the blessings of the Light and *Receive for the Self Alone*. But along this path, we become complacent, protective, insular, reactive, self-satisfied, and ultimately filled with fear of any change.

Or, alternatively, we can take advantage of the force of judgment present during this month/sign, engage with the world, and discover what was previously unknown to us. We can transform our *Desire to Receive for the Self Alone* to a *Desire to Receive for the Sake of Sharing*. We can emerge from our bubble and see the world for what it is, make judgments, take action, and be sensitive to others. We can engage the world and all its problems, even if it means losing some of our own peace and tranquility. Taureans can risk change without fear.

IF YOUR *TIKKUN* (CORRECTION) IS
IN TAURUS...

This is one of the most difficult corrections to make. Those who have their *tikkun* in Taurus were Scorpios in a previous incarnation. Scorpio is the sign of self-destruction. In this lifetime, it is likely that the hurdle of a self-destructive nature remains to be overcome.

At some point in this life or a past life, you were probably the victim of some deliberate injustice. You may have been robbed or driven out of your home. As a result, you carry feelings of anger and distrust. You may go to extraordinary lengths to hold onto your possessions when you sense, accurately or not, that someone is about to take them from you. You would rather destroy your own belongings than have them fall into others' hands. This applies to relationships as well as material possessions.

Fear of repeating your past life may hamper your growth in this one. Despite this self-destructive tendency, your social behavior is friendly and spontaneous. Though still a rebel at heart, in this lifetime you are constrained by your own anxiety.

Your supernatural powers have not always been used in a positive way, but this time these gifts will help you reach elevated levels of consciousness—as long as they are used in the service of others and toward more constructive goals.

The *tikkun* in Taurus also reveals an individual whose attitude toward sex is relatively unbalanced. You are passionate, with a large sexual appetite that has caused many upheavals in your life, traces of which are still to be found in your present life.

To avoid revisiting the situations you experienced as a Scorpio, you must overcome your residual fears, distrust, and anger. To achieve this goal, your *tikkun* directs you toward the positive aspects of Taurus's Light: to appreciate the beauty and pleasures of this life and, in so doing, banish fear, distrust, and anger. This new approach to the world will let you express yourself without the anxiety induced by fear of losing your possessions.

Taurus's Light is a blessing that will open you to the wonders of this world. Letting in the Light of Taurus pushes out the Scorpio darkness. If you succeed in breaking out of this Scorpio envelope, you can **transform your need for immediate gratification into a true gift for generosity, which will lead you to come near to a total correction:** *divine love*. This will enable you to transform your reactive belligerence into proactive serenity. By enjoying life, you can renew it and reclaim it. Your former torments will be appeased by your newfound peace.

THIS MONTH'S INFLUENCE ON ALL OF US:

Fulfillment

Often, we relinquish control of our lives to doctors, lawyers, and other "experts," expecting them to heal our physical, financial, and emotional wounds. However, true healing and fulfillment is our own responsibility. This spiritual truth is made more evident this month as the effulgent Light radiating in *Iyar* inspires us to seek healing and fulfillment from within.

THE MONTH OF *SIVAN* (GEMINI)

Searching for the "There" There

Sivan is the third month of the lunar calendar, ruled by the planet Mercury, which is named after the Roman messenger of the gods. In Aramaic, Mercury is called *Chochav*, which is associated both with communication in the physical world and with integration of the physical and spiritual dimensions.

The Aramaic letters that connect us to the spiritual energy of the month are *Reish* ‏ר‎, which created the planet Mercury, and *Zayin* ‏ז‎, which created the sign of Gemini, or the Twins. Together they tell us that *Sivan* is a month filled with potential for unification, particularly for the fusion of the physical and spiritual worlds.

"Quick" is the word that comes up most often when thinking about Gemini—quick to judge, quick to react, and quick to change. Quick as in clever and lively, but also quick as in momentary, superficial, and passing. In this little word, all the strengths and weaknesses of the month/sign begin to emerge.

Geminis are worthy representatives of Mercury, the fastest planet in the solar system, which makes its trip around the sun in a mere 88 days. That's 104,000 miles per hour—almost twice as fast as the earth.

Like the planet that rules them, Geminis are speedballs. While most people require time to absorb information before taking action, Geminis seem to gather information and react to it simultaneously. If they see it, they "get" it, and they're on the move. They have a remarkable ability to grasp all sides of a question, synthesize viewpoints, and come to a decision almost at once. In this, they take advantage of the inherent duality of the sign. They see things with more than one set of eyes, sometimes even seeming to be in two places at once.

It's not easy to have the last word with Geminis, because they have an answer for everything and possess extraordinary powers of persuasion. They hold their own opinions in very high regard—unless, of course, they happen to change their minds. Geminis can contradict themselves in a fraction of second, not because they were seduced by an interesting argument, but because a new perspective is sufficiently attractive for them to want to take credit for it. Though not materialistic in the ordinary sense of the word, they are what might be called "intellectually" materialistic. Ideas are Geminis' coins, and they like to collect, count, rearrange, and spend them. They also could be called intellectual opportunists. If an idea works, they use it. If not, they toss it aside.

Geminis are extraordinary communicators, quickly getting to the heart of even the most complex issues. Yet their own hearts present them with their greatest challenges. Because they move so quickly, Geminis may have difficulty staying still long enough for anything to really touch them. They are not models of perseverance. They may start a new job or a new relationship with great enthusiasm, only to leave it after a short period of time. By not persevering, Geminis deprive themselves of any meaningful enjoyment. They may waste energy concealing their ignorance rather than applying it to master a subject. They may use their mental agility to escape emotional discomfort. They may skim the surface of an idea or a relationship and miss its real significance.

The *Book of Formation* reveals that the organs of the body that relate to Geminis are the lungs and the nervous system. When a Gemini becomes disconnected from the "big picture" by being too quick to judge, they weaken their link with the Upper World, and this can make them prone to bouts of pneumonia and bronchitis.

So Geminis are curious, creative, friendly, multitalented, intelligent, and open. But they can also be flighty, fickle, impatient, restless, anxious, snappish, sarcastic, gossipy, and cynical. Are they simply fast-talking, charmingly persuasive, and quick-witted entertainers? Or is there something more to them—perhaps even much more?

In kabbalistic astrology, the strengths and weaknesses of a month/sign are cut from the same cloth. We refer to this idea as a double-edged sword that could cut in two very distinct and opposite ways. At their worst, Geminis are like quicksilver—hard to catch, hard to pin down. If you've ever broken a thermometer, you know what we're talking about. Like quicksilver, Geminis tend to fluctuate wildly depending on the temperature around them, molding themselves to any situation without a form or identity of their own.

Geminis try to find themselves by adapting, like a chameleon, to whatever colors surround them, hoping to blend in. But their real identity can't be found outside themselves. Satisfaction comes only from a deeper approach to ideas, to relationships, to themselves, to life.

Fortunately, they are not without the tools to accomplish this. The opportunity is there for the taking.

Mercury, the ruler of Gemini and the month of *Sivan*, is the planet nearest to the sun, our source of light and energy. In kabbalistic astrology, physical proximity indicates a spiritual resemblance. As the closest planet to the sun, Mercury has the greatest spiritual similarity to that star. As you might expect, the sun represents a spiritual dimension above the physical world that we inhabit, a world connected more directly to the Light that made us. Mercury shares this potential connection with the Light. And if the planet shares it, so does the month/sign.

How can we take advantage of this affinity?

Geminis can be very positive channels for the Light—if they use their gifts for communication in a sharing way. They have the ability to absorb, analyze, and transmit vast amounts of information and to communicate at many levels. But they must learn to linger a little longer over things if they want to get at the truth. To get there, they must understand that our own minds are not the source of our gifts. The Light is the source. Our abilities and gifts are the blessings of the Light.

To maximize these blessings, Geminis must use them in a sharing way. They must go beyond a transitory intellectual self-stimulation. They must allow ideas and people to touch them, and resist the urge to flee at the slightest twinge of emotional or intellectual discomfort. To connect with the world, they must penetrate beneath appearances. In this way, they will become true messengers of the Light, creating links between ideas, between themselves and others, and, ultimately, between this world and the Upper World.

IF YOUR *TIKKUN* (CORRECTION) IS IN GEMINI...

If you have a *tikkun* in Gemini, you formerly had the characteristics of a Sagittarius. This means that you behaved like a disorganized and spoiled child, living from hand to mouth, guided mainly by selfish desires. As a Sagittarius, you cared little for the people around you or what they thought. Married, you behaved as though you were single.

The satisfaction of your own immediate needs dominated your whole life. Your thirst for knowledge and study led you to discover new horizons, but in the end you remained a prisoner of your own desires. You lived an active life and did whatever you wanted to do, but you could not commit yourself to any cause that was not directly concerned with your own immediate interests. Serving others and taking their needs into consideration seemed to restrict you. Hungry for freedom, ignoring social constraints, you eagerly sought justice, but for yourself alone. You neither cooperated with your fellow human beings nor gave them much credit.

But sharing does not restrain your freedom; it enhances it. By opening yourself up to the needs of others in this life, you will overcome the leftover self-absorption that has hindered your spiritual transformation. By communicating openly, you can experience deeper fulfillment than you were able to find in the limited immediate pleasures that you settled for in your previous life, and receive the benefit that the Light wants to share with all of us. To do this, you must learn to conduct yourself with humility and become more respectful toward those around you.

Following this path will lead to a transformation of your abilities. Your curiosity will give you access to the surrounding world, but this time through the sharing of knowledge. By doing this, you will find new and more profound meaning in your working life and in your most intimate relationships. You will understand that a true and lasting freedom is forged from your connections to others and from an exchange of ideas that lead to a true metamorphosis!

THIS MONTH'S INFLUENCE ON ALL OF US:

Relationships

For the rest of us, the potential of the month is clear. In life, we always want the most in the least amount of time. But the month of Sivan gives us the unique opportunity to go beyond the surface of the physical world and reveal the deeper spiritual meaning hidden within.

For all of us, this is a month to focus on developing relationships with others and with the spiritual elements of ourselves. This is a time to form lasting unions, such as marriages, and is particularly suited to thoughtful reflection on ways to integrate the "twins" of the physical and spiritual worlds that live in all of us.

THE MONTH OF *TAMMUZ* (CANCER)

Ever-Changing Moon

*T*ammuz is the only month/sign ruled by the moon, which in Kabbalah represents the feminine principle in the universe. The moon is also associated with *Malchut*, the physical world of manifestation and finality, doubt, and limitation. The symbol of the sign is the Crab.

The Aramaic letters that connect us to the spiritual energy of the month are *Tav* תַּ, which created the Moon, and *Chet* חֵ, which created the sign of Cancer. *Tav* is the last letter of the Aramaic alphabet and generally indicates endings, limitations, and borders. *Chet* is a very interesting letter because it is made by combining the *Zayin* זֵ of Gemini with the *Vav* וֵ of Taurus. Taken together, the letters tell us that we can overcome the negative influences of this month by combining the positive aspects of the two previous months.

The Zohar teaches us that the three most "negative" months of the year are *Tammuz* (Cancer), *Av* (Leo), and *Tevet* (Capricorn). In kabbalistic astrology, the term *negative* refers to judgment. During these months, we find that judgment is more direct. There is less mercy in the universe, less time between cause and effect, and less time between actions and their consequences.

Cancer, or *Sartan* in Aramaic, is one of only two signs that receive the full influence of the heavenly bodies ruling them. The remaining ten signs are governed by five planets; each sign shares the energy of its ruling planet with one other sign. For example, Venus influences both Taurus and Libra; Mercury influences both Gemini and Virgo. Cancer, however, is the only sign ruled by the moon, and because of this, the moon's energy is purely and completely manifested in Cancer. The moon's influence is magnified even further because Cancer is a water sign, and we all know how the pull of gravity is responsible for the oceans' tides.

To understand the sign of Cancer, then, we begin by considering the moon, the symbol of variability and our planet's closest neighbor. Each and every night, the moon shows us a different face. With such a changeable ruling planet, Cancer's feelings of instability, uncertainty, and insecurity should come as no surprise. Nor should we be surprised at Cancer's attempts to regain security and stability by seeking reassurance in material comforts. Cancers are like the children of unpredictable and inconsistent parents: Such children compensate for their lack of security by becoming cautious, apprehensive, and acquisitive. Like their symbol, the Crab, Cancers may create a protective shell of material things to shield them from what seems to be a capricious and uncertain world.

Cancers often have round faces. The weak point of their body is their fragile stomach—they have a difficult digestive system and may be susceptible to ulcers. Cancers also have a tendency to suffer emotionally. They are prone to depression and severe mood swings—from joy to sadness to anger, and back again within seconds. On the positive side, this hypersensitivity allows them to understand quickly what others need or want. Cancers are keen observers of every movement or gesture, tirelessly looking for hints of change or trouble. They are extremely intuitive.

But they are also extremely vulnerable. Because of this, they are constantly torn between their understanding of others' needs and their own need to protect themselves. Therefore, they may retreat into a shell, hiding behind a mask of seeming indifference. Fear of hurt may immobilize them and prevent them from taking any action that could benefit someone else or themselves.

Kabbalah associates the moon with *Malchut*, the physical world we see, hear, taste, smell, and touch. But in the physical world, we are limited by physical laws. We are limited by time. We are limited by our own bodies. Death is present in the physical world.

Since there is no apparent way around these endings and limitations, we develop strategies for working within the finite system.

Cancers, however, being under the influence of the moon, often feel that they cannot deal with the limitations that the physical world presents. Unlike Taureans, Cancers feel that they have no comforting Light to escape into. For Cancers, the finite and apparently predetermined aspects of the physical world are a constant worrisome companion. They find themselves looking for the negativity that lurks everywhere, and it's no surprise that they usually find it.

For Cancers, things are always about to come to an end. They may become reluctant to take risks. They may fear being misjudged, and constantly seek reassurance and recognition. Taken to extremes, this anxiety can paralyze them. The future terrifies them. The past, on the other hand, is reassuring, and they recall it with great delight. They may even seek refuge in the past, stubbornly refusing to abandon its cocoon-like security.

But remember, limitations, finality, endings, restrictions, doubt, and death are all illusions. Kabbalah tells us that the physical world is the seeable, hearable, smellable, touchable, and tastable form of the hidden spiritual worlds.

Malchut, the physical world, represents the physical dimension where there are endings, doubt, and death. If Cancers are full of anguish and fear, it is only to the extent that they invest their energy in the illusion of *Malchut*.

Kabbalah tells us that our five senses perceive no more than 5% of reality. When we base our understanding and judgments solely on this 5%, it should come as no surprise that we are filled with hesitation and doubt. By excluding 95% of reality from our awareness, we miss the underlying spiritual truth of all Creation.

What are the positive aspects of Cancer?

Here's what the Aramaic letters tell us. *Chet* is constructed of *Vav* and *Zayin*. *Vav* is a force of healing that connects us to the Upper Worlds. It represents sharing, unity, love, and balance. *Zayin* is a sword with the power to elevate reality to a higher and purer level.

The month of *Tammuz* gives us the opportunity to regain our balance, unify our lives, heal ourselves, and overcome the apparent limitations of the physical world through the use of sharing and love. By doing so, we are able to see beyond the physical world to the Upper Worlds.

For Cancers in particular, this means taking a more long-term view. You must emerge from your armor of material possessions and your masks of indifference, and expose yourself to risk. To do this, you must recognize that the light of the moon may be uncertain and changeable, but the Light we are made of is everlasting. You must release your talents for empathy and intuitive understanding into the world. Share it with others, not for the sake of recognition, but for its own sake.

Nothing will help you more to overcome your inclination toward depression and anxiety than sharing with others and putting into practice your enormous potential for generosity.

By doing this, you will begin to look beyond *Malchut* and forge a genuine connection to the spiritual world. Remember, the only riches truly capable of satisfying us are not material. Love, health, security, and even power are humankind's deepest aspirations, and these are all metaphysical concepts, not material objects.

IF YOUR *TIKKUN* (CORRECTION) IS IN CANCER...

The person with a *tikkun* in Cancer carries an enormous amount of pride left over from a previous incarnation as a Capricorn. As a Capricorn, you were totally obsessed with professional victory, honor, and respectability. Bolstering your own reputation was the main motivation of your life. You undertook impossible tasks, if only to gain the admiration of others. You appointed yourself judge and jury and, as a consequence, condemned the mistakes committed by others.

Though you saw yourself as a guardian of the moral order, you neglected morality's most important attribute—mercy. As a result, you have not forged many friendships and have often been considered a shameless opportunist. This drive to achieve overwhelmed you with excessive responsibilities that prevented you from thinking of others. Consumed by social missions, you were, oddly enough, oblivious to other people. You lived cut off from the real pleasures of life—home, family, friendship—and lived a secluded, selfish existence in your own secret universe.

From this previous incarnation, you have the seriousness and discipline to accomplish whatever goals you set for yourself in this life. But the *tikkun* in Cancer suggests that you relinquish the notion that professional victories, social importance, and your own reputation are the keys to your happiness. Kabbalistic wisdom tells us that these are all illusions.

Your correction in Cancer points you toward a new goal. It suggests that real happiness—durable, satisfying happiness—can be found in the creation of a truly warm and loving home. Along this path, you will discover a world heretofore unknown to you is filled with the wonder, simplicity, and spontaneity of childhood. You will learn flexibility and generosity in relationships and parenthood.

The most difficult renunciation of your past life will lie in your abandonment of the well-established Capricorn ideas of success and failure. **The key to your real success will be found in the loving eyes of your family and in your dedication and devotion to that love.** It is here that you will find the ultimate satisfaction.

THIS MONTH'S INFLUENCE ON
ALL OF US:

Healing

T he physical and spiritual disease of cancer is born in *Tammuz*; hence the name "Cancer." Cancer can occur in business, relationships, and the physical body. *The Zohar*, however, explains that before a disease is created, the antidote and cure originate first. This month is our antidote and proactive healing process. We should direct our consciousness toward healing throughout this period. Strive more to ensure that all your actions and deeds embody care and tolerance for others. Maintain your connection to the Light to ensure health and well-being in all areas of your life.

THE MONTH OF *AV* (LEO)

Breaking the Pride of Lions

*A*v is the fifth month on the lunar calendar, and it is the only month/sign ruled by the sun, which in Kabbalah represents the masculine aspect in the universe. *Av* means father. Its symbol is the lion, one of the four Holy Entities, the other three being the Bull (Taurus), the Eagle, and Mankind. *The Zohar* explains that energy descends from the Upper Worlds into our world through these four entities.

The Aramaic letters that connect us to the spiritual energy of the month are *Caf* כ, which created the sun, and *Tet* ט, which created the sign of Leo. *Caf* represents the Crown, royalty, balance, and completeness. *Tet* represents the sexual organ. This is generally understood as a dual potential for either bliss, or destruction, ecstasy or misery.

Leos receive their energy directly from the sun, and they are the only sign that falls under its influence. Because of this, Leos believe that the whole world revolves around them.

Confident of their power and abilities, they broadcast their self-assurance to the whole world. And they are hard to ignore. Their appearance is generally stately and impressive, sometimes even intimidating, and they tend to be the center of attention. They may behave like benevolent but omnipotent royalty out for a walk among their loyal subjects. Leos demand respect, and if they are treated otherwise, they will either retaliate or dismiss the insignificant peasant as though they were shooing away a fly. Like kings or queens, they can be arrogant and disdainful. They are not like the rest of us. They are Leos!

Leos' weak point is the heart, and they are prone to cardiovascular disease. Kabbalah tells us that a Leo's role in the world is comparable to the heart's role in the body. Both have been given the responsibility of pumping out and distributing all the energy that they receive.

Leos do not place their trust easily, but when they do, they choose companions and counsel wisely. They tend, however, to rely completely on themselves. They seldom ask for help, because they don't feel they really need it. And even if they do ask, they don't really listen to others' advice. In their view, colleagues and friends are not helpmates or equals; their function is to do Leo's bidding, like a rock star's entourage. And despite the fact that they themselves are poor listeners, Leos are never shy about dispensing advice to others. They can even be heavy-handed and dictatorial, like authoritarian parents who feel they are surrounded by innocent and inexperienced children.

As natural leaders, Leos like to organize those around them, even when no one has asked to be organized. This is why we find many Leos in politics, education, and corporate leadership. Leos are always looking for a kingdom to rule. Their enormous *Desire to Receive* urges them to want everything they see and to take charge of every situation they encounter. They handle stress well, are goal oriented, and are generous and impartial in their dealings with their subordinates. They are, however, susceptible to flattery, which induces them to reward those who acknowledge them while ignoring those who may show indifference. A few well-placed compliments will turn a Leo's head. Put another way, Leos can be bought! The sun is the earth's source of energy. Without it, life would not exist. In Kabbalah, the sun links us to the Infinite Light, the spiritual energy that made us and that contains everything positive. It is during the month of *Av* that this energy is most abundantly present in the universe.

But *Av* is still considered one of the three most negative months. In Kabbalah, the more positive the energy available in the universe, the stronger the negativity can be. The brighter the sun, the greater the potential for sunburn and drought. So while the sun can give life, it can also destroy. Kabbalistic wisdom tells us that the month of *Av* is negative, but only to the extent that we are unable to channel its powerful constructive energy. As long as we ourselves remain constructive and proactive, we can be an effective channel for the enormous positive energy manifested in the universe during this time.

In order to act positively, **Leos must come to understand that they are neither the center of the universe nor even the kings of the savannah. Leos have been blessed with great power in order to be guides on the path to enlightenment.** They were not blessed with generosity, strength, honesty, charisma, and creativity to satisfy their own egos. They do not "deserve" their gifts any more than a bird "deserves" its wings. They are given these gifts to share and care for others and to assist them in making their corrections, their *tikkun*. If they want to keep their privileged position, they must use their gifts selflessly and fight the delusion that their earthly gifts are the product of their own genius.

Again, as we said of Geminis: Your own mind is not the source of your gifts. The Light is the source. Your abilities are the blessings of the Light.

Unfortunately for Leos, the greater their abilities, the stronger their delusion is. Pride is the culprit. Because of this, throughout their lives, Leos face situations that put their pride to the test.

To overcome this obstacle, Leos must not pursue honor or respect—because nothing is owed to them! Only the Light gives you what you have. You have created nothing by yourself, so there is no justification for vanity when you succeed. The Light is everywhere and for everyone. Leos must share the energy that has been granted them. You must be attentive to others and open to the possibility that someone else's opinion may have merit. The true measure of Leos is revealed by their sharing deeds. If you give help anonymously, without looking for personal benefit or glow, then and only then will you have overcome pride.

More than any other sign, Leos' generosity must be totally altruistic. Nothing you give belongs to you anyway. Your only true choice concerns the motivation for your actions: Is it for the self alone, or is it in order to share?

IF YOUR *TIKKUN* (CORRECTION) IS IN LEO...

The person with a *tikkun* in Leo carries the former life of an Aquarius into this life. You are an individual who is set apart. In your previous incarnation, you were considered important and unique, and you have brought tremendous inner power, ample creativity, and fierce ambition with you into this life. You were never a model of discipline, however, and you still seek originality at any cost. You are a rule breaker. As a result, you may have difficulty getting others to take you seriously.

Although keeping yourself apart has strengthened you, you overcame doubts by confronting them. Relationships meant the world to you, but you were always afraid of being abandoned. You even tolerated abuse in order to maintain closeness, and you always had the feeling of not receiving in return for what you had given. You let relationships dominate you, and because of this, you never developed to your full spiritual potential.

In your previous incarnation, you had the opportunity to rise from abject poverty to the heights of affluence, and these opportunities will present themselves again in your present incarnation—if you learn to exploit your inner strength. You have been severely scarred by your lack of discipline, which in previous incarnations prevented you from focusing on real goals. In your life as an Aquarius, you already had an acute sense of justice and equality. Your energy was utilized now and again for defending noble causes, but you preferred to deal with masses of people rather than with individual human beings. You see yourself in the future rather than in the present.

The *tikkun* in Leo points you toward abandoning desire for superficial originality in favor of developing your capacity to serve humanity. You must pursue this path for yourself, not for the eyes of others. You have, in fact, more than one key from your previous incarnation to use in this one. Your ambition will help you find a true and noble cause through which you will share your gifts with humanity. **Your *tikkun* suggests that you will be given the opportunity to lead, provided that you do so in a selfless way. Along this path, you can use your inner strength, creativity, and originality to reveal new opportunities in the world around you.**

THIS MONTH'S INFLUENCE ON ALL OF US:

Ego

O ur ego constantly convinces us that we know it all—that we alone are the architects of our own success. Humility is therefore the key word of the month. Go out and ask for help—from the Light and especially from people with whom you feel competitive.

THE MONTH OF *ELUL* (VIRGO)

Proud Mary

Ruled by the planet Mercury, the sign of Virgo in the month of *Elul* is the sixth and last of the "masculine" months/signs—the final month in which everything is in its potential or "seed-level" state. *Elul* grants us the opportunity to modify the next six "feminine" months. During this month, we can use Virgo's influence to take stock of ourselves, identify our faults, and "clean house." For this reason, *Elul* is called the Month of Repentance.

"Virgo" denotes virginity and purity.

The Aramaic letters that connect us to the spiritual energy of this month are *Yud* **ﬗ**, which created the sign of Virgo, and *Reish* **ﬧ** , which created the planet Mercury. These two letters have diametrically opposed energy intelligences. *Yud* symbolizes richness and the highest level of consciousness. *Reish* is the image of poverty. During the month of *Elul*, we should take advantage of the opportunity to unify these two concepts and balance their energies.

Virgo, like Gemini, is ruled by the planet Mercury. Those born under both signs have the ability to adapt quickly to new situations and ideas, but a Virgo doesn't shift viewpoints with the same eagerness as a Gemini. Both are likely to jump to hasty conclusions, but they base their decisions on different factors.

Physically, Virgos are often long-legged and slim. Their weak point is the digestive system and the intestines.

Virgos' main characteristic is their perpetual quest for order and perfection. Nothing disturbs a Virgo more than untidiness. Their desks, their homes, and their cars are examples of efficiency and neatness—for a Virgo, everything has a prescribed place. Virgos are reliable and responsible, and it is a point of honor for them to complete each task they are given. To Virgos, the physical world requires perfect order, which they have been put on earth to maintain. With their commitment to accuracy and precision, they are well represented among copy editors, accountants, and surgeons.

No other sign has Virgo's analytical, logical, and methodical capabilities. But their perfectionism prevents them from grasping the bigger picture. Their view of the world may become reduced to a single grain of sand, when an entire beach should be taken into account.

In their quest for perfection, Virgos quickly focus on the inadequacies and errors of those around them. They are seldom diplomatic or tactful, and often lack the sensitivity required for a meaningful exchange of ideas. It's not that they intend to hurt others; errors and imperfections insult their sense of order, and they lash out to rectify the flaws as quickly as possible. Virgos believe that their abilities authorize them to comment on and criticize others as they see fit. At the same time, however, they tend to consider themselves above reproach. In this respect, they mimic the unassailable Virgin of their sign. Although they are able to mix easily with all classes of people, they can be almost unbearably proud.

Virgo is an earth sign, and a Virgo's view of the world is physical and practical. But because of this, theirs is a limited view. Virgos see only a fraction of the whole picture. They seldom question "why," only "how." By nature, Virgos are not very spiritual. To develop their spiritual potential, they must see beyond the physicality of the world. And for a Virgo, this is a tall order.

In order to move toward a corrected life, Virgos must first understand that the world that our five senses reveals is limited because it represents only a small portion of reality. The greater part of reality resides in the spiritual world. Once Virgos accept this, they will realize that they are able to see the small details only because the Light has allowed them to do so.

We've said this before, but it bears repeating: Your own mind is not the source of your gifts. The Light is the source. You are the Vessel. If you want to be a source of Light, you have to share your gifts.

Virgos must learn to focus their critical eye on themselves
first, and not assume that their conclusions are absolute
truths. When you feel compelled to criticize or pass judgment
on something or someone, you should first ask yourself, "Do
I see the whole picture, or is there something I have missed?"
By holding back, by restricting this initial impulse, Virgos can
escape their own shortsightedness and begin to see the larger
picture. Virgos who want to correct themselves must refrain
from giving advice to others until they have questioned their
own motives.

More than any other sign, Virgos must resist passing judgment based on first impressions. If, for example, untidiness or
a lack of order has simply aggravated their own narrow sense
of order, then their intervention is clearly for the *Self Alone*
and hence not constructive. On the other hand, if they want
to offer advice or assistance out of genuine concern for someone else's welfare, then and only then may they do so, because
it is in the name of sharing. As usual, motivation is the key.

As the Month of Repentance, *Elul* is particularly suited to an
examination of our past, taking stock of ourselves, and making amends for past misdeeds. How can we best accomplish
this?

Kabbalah teaches that if we have harmed someone, whether
intentionally or not, we are held responsible only for our own
actions, since the injured person was clearly destined to have
that experience, whether by our actions or by someone else's.

What we have done by our harmful actions was act as a channel or an agent of the negativity that was due to the victim. We haven't exactly done them any favors, but Kabbalah recognizes that the Light works in mysterious ways. Thieves are guilty for their offenses, but according to Kabbalah, the victims of the theft were meant to have that experience of loss. **In other words, we are not responsible for the victim's destiny, but we are responsible for our own destiny, which allowed us to become the channel for negativity.**

Because of this, the only way to truly repent is to change the future by returning to the past. Simply apologizing profusely for a past offense will not change anything, nor will it relieve the pain that the victim feels. To repent, you must go back, understand what caused you to act badly, admit your mistake, and request that the same situation occur again in the future so that you will have an opportunity to act differently, thereby enabling you to make your correction.

The energy of the month of Virgo offers us the opportunity to examine ourselves thoroughly. This is the reason the sign is Virgo: It has the power to purify, to cleanse the world of its imperfections.

IF YOUR *TIKKUN* (CORRECTION) IS IN VIRGO...

L ike the Piscean you were in your former life, you have been consumed by your dreams and fantasies and have paid dearly for your melodramatic inclinations. Nourished on tragic stories, you totally lacked the capacity to discern between right and wrong, between good and bad. Confronted with numerous obstacles, you often just let things happen. When they didn't work out, you succumbed to self-pity.

In your previous life, you were heavily dependent on others. But your sensitivity to pain inhibited you from relieving that pain. This same emotional fragility may have led you to seek refuge in drugs or alcohol or other head-in-the-sand behaviors. Your intuition may have allowed you to act for others with the intention of helping them, but you were never completely free of a sort of self-interest. You had talent in the arts and you could have been a famous musician or painter. Many of your "good deeds" were a pretext for receiving gratitude.

To make your correction, you must gain a more realistic and less hypersensitive view of the world. You must use more reason and less emotion in making your decisions. Self-discipline and determination will help keep your feet on the ground and extract you from overly dependent relationships. Most of all, you must stop letting things happen to you by taking responsibility for yourself. You must learn to speak your mind both for your own benefit and for others. Essentially, you must stop whining.

This lifetime affords you an opportunity to settle accounts, forgive, and move on. Reflection will be your new tool for tackling problems, but action will put you on the road to your correction. If you succeed in establishing values within yourself and get your head out of the melodramatic clouds, you will be able to turn your attention toward creating.

If you succeed in establishing more concrete values, detach yourself from emotions, gain independence from those around you, and stick with your desires long enough, you will know love and inner peace. This will help you to seize opportunities, overcome obstacles, and manifest your dreams in the real world. Preserving relationships at all costs and always compromising have not proven to be the right solution for you. Your new motto should be "here and now." This will help you to seize opportunities, overcome obstacles, and manifest your dreams in the real world.

THIS MONTH'S INFLUENCE ON ALL OF US:

Spiritual Cleansing

This month grants us the opportunity to alter our destiny in the next six months. Look inward. Identify your faults. Uproot your immoral traits. Eradicate self-centered habits. In other words, "clean house." Proactive spiritual work and purification during this month will have a direct impact on the measure and radiance of Light that you'll ignite the rest of the year.

THE MONTH OF *TISHREI* (LIBRA)

None of the Above

The sign of Libra in the month of *Tishrei* is ruled, like Taurus, by the planet Venus. Libra is the seventh month/sign, and the first in the second half of the yearly cycle. These final six months of the year are considered "feminine" months and are seen as the visible expression of what has already been planted by the "seeds" of the six "masculine" months. Librans are represented by the Scales, which symbolize justice, equilibrium, and balance.

The Aramaic letters that connect us to the spiritual energy of the month are *Lamed* ל, which created the sign of Libra, and *Pei* פ, which created the planet Venus. *Lamed* is the only letter of the Aramaic alphabet to extend above the writing line, which indicates that Libra's source of energy is drawn from a superior world and is directly linked to this higher energy plane. Therefore, **this is considered an excellent month for taking action.**

The energy intelligence of Venus can be so overwhelmingly
bright that it blurs distinctions between good and bad. For
Taureans, this brightness often results in their assuming that
all is well with the world, that negativity and darkness don't
exist at all, and that they may therefore cut themselves off
from the world's problems. For Librans, on the other hand,
the light of Venus seems to make all things equal, and this
often leads to uncertainty and indecisiveness. Making decisions or judgments presents difficulties to both Taureans and
Librans. For Taureans it is a case of "won't;" they don't want
to make a judgment. For Librans, however, it is a case of
"can't"—they seem unable to decide between two equally
weighted sides.

According to the *Book of Formation*, the organs of the body
that relate to Librans are the ears and the kidneys. The ears
denote balance, and the kidneys correspond to the emotions.
Though Librans strive for equilibrium, balance, and harmony
in their relationships and environments, they usually find
themselves in a state of confusion. They mull things over,
obsessively considering every angle of an issue in an attempt
to reach equanimity. They perpetually hesitate, wavering
between one aspect or the other. Librans always see both
sides of an argument, and both sides seem to hold equal
merit. They become paralyzed with the fear of making a mistake or a bad choice. They often make decisions by default.
They say to themselves, "I have an opportunity to change
something here, to reveal a great deal of Light—if I make the
right choice. But how do I know if this is the right answer?
There might be another point of view, a different truth."

Librans rarely take decisive action. When they do, they may find themselves moving in fits and starts, retracing their steps, and revisiting old decisions filled with an anxiety that they have neglected to fully consider each and every possibility. Librans can never "leave well enough alone." They will go through periods of strenuous activity and make great progress, but as soon as the pressure diminishes, they become uncertain again and may proceed to undo what they have already accomplished. They can turn even the simplest problem into a quagmire of doubt and ambiguity.

Librans can be very social. They are friendly, open, warm, sympathetic to others' problems, and they encourage others to confide in them. They enjoy caring for others, and as soon as someone shows the slightest need, a Libran will be there to lend a hand. If you are not a Libran and are seeking advice, Librans can be particularly good sounding boards, because they give equal weight to all possibilities. Just don't ask a Libran to make a decision for you. You will be inundated with pluses and minuses, pros and cons, advantages and disadvantages, but no conclusions.

Although Venus is the planet of love, Librans' relationships clearly reflect their indecisiveness. Uncertainty undermines their commitments. This uncertainty is connected to their self-image—Librans cannot even make clear determinations about themselves. Lacking a clearly defined sense of purpose or self-worth, you often seek security in relationships. But you have difficulty giving yourself to someone entirely. Your loyalties are always divided, your relationships rarely complete. To a Libran, everything, even love, warrants a self-interrogation. "Am I right to love this person? Is he or she worthy of my affection?" Afraid of being hurt, you tell yourself that there are good reasons for not loving someone wholeheartedly, and that by restraining your feelings, you are protecting yourself.

Despite good intentions, Librans excessively rationalize and always find intellectual justification for their doubts. Librans seem frozen in time. They evade confrontation, avoid responsibility, and refuse to tackle their problems. Pride won't allow them to make a decision that could prove to be in error.

Librans want to solve everything rationally. They believe in their own intellectual abilities and want to reveal the truth by using them. They fail to recognize that spiritual truth is beyond human logic.

The Light has an eternal *Desire to Share* its blessings, but there must be a Vessel to receive this gift. The Light we receive is exactly equal to our *Desire to Receive* it. The Light does not give us any less, nor any more, than we desire.

Because of their pride and their reliance on logic, Librans resist the blessings of the Light. **In order to correct themselves, Librans must learn to trust the Light and must understand that making mistakes is one of the ways we grow. Librans simply must take action in order to reveal the Light.** For them, deliberation is merely a diversion that impedes action. Good intentions are not enough. To make progress, Librans must overcome their fear of failure and stop seeking logical solutions. If they are open and give themselves to positive activities unconditionally, the Light will not let them down.

In other words, they should just "jump in." The water's fine.

IF YOUR *TIKKUN* (CORRECTION) IS IN LIBRA...

I n your previous incarnation as an Aries, you were noted for self-confidence, but your high opinion of yourself led to many disappointments. Preoccupied with yourself, you wasted your energy and were in an almost constant state of agitation. Although you worked, you never built anything solid. You overreacted to failures, assumed aggressive attitudes, and often grappled with problems in very narrow-minded ways. This brought about a profound sense of frustration, which in your present life has provoked an aggressiveness that often puzzles those close to you.

A *tikkun* in Libra points you toward sacrifice in its noblest sense. To free yourself from frustration, you need to move along a path of devotion to a cause beyond yourself. In the past, your ego placed you within a limited circle of friends, which restricted your opportunities for sharing. Being a part of a team will help you regain equilibrium. As part of a team, you will need to consider what others say and open yourself to the possibility that their opinions have merit. This will soften your personality, and you will become more capable of mastering your anger.

As you come to understand that the group's success is more important than your own, you will experience real happiness. Through this sort of unselfishness, you can accomplish your correction and find inner peace.

The *tikkun* in Libra is one of the more difficult corrections, because it entails nullifying your pride in this life in order to correct the errors of a previous one. Your previous antisocial behavior put pressure on relationships, making you go through emotional breakdowns. You have never known durable relationships. For this purpose, your marriage will provide the best opportunity to understand real sharing and gain inner strength from loving someone else selflessly. By becoming the driving force behind your partner, you will be able to let go of your narrow idea of "*I*" and begin to move through the world as "*we*." At the same time, you'll come to understand that the goal is less important than the process of achieving it, and this new perspective will reveal new horizons.

THIS MONTH'S INFLUENCE ON
ALL OF US:

New Beginnings

Tishrei is the beginning and seed level of the new year. *Rosh Hashanah*, *Yom Kippur*, and *Succoth* occur in this month. It is a time of reflection, self-examination, and accountability. Any hardships or negativity that we experienced over the last year illustrates that the seeds planted a year ago required more care, purity, and commitment on our part. Think about digging deeper this year. Put forth more effort. The purer the seed you plant this month, the sweeter and more abundant the fruits will be in the year to come.

THE MONTH OF *MAR-CHESHVAN* (SCORPIO)

A Bitter Tail

Mar-Cheshvan is the eighth month on the lunar calendar. Like Aries, it is ruled by the planet Mars, named after the Roman god of war. The symbol for the month/sign is the Scorpion. The letters that connect us to the spiritual energy of the month are *Dalet* ד, which created Mars, and *Nun* נ, which created the sign of Scorpio. Together, these two letters form the Aramaic word *Din*, which means "judgment." Judgment can be cruel, harsh, and unfeeling. It can burn like fire. Combined with mercy, however, judgment has great healing potential.

When you meet a Scorpio, you can feel his or her energy and know immediately that you are in the presence of a person to be reckoned with. Scorpios emanate powerful magnetism while at the same time appearing cold and reserved. They can be charming, bewitching, and even hypnotizing. In their presence, you feel attraction but also uneasiness.

Scorpio is ruled by Mars, but this does not mean that Scorpios are courageous. It does mean that the mere idea of confrontation gets a Scorpio's blood up. As soon as Scorpios sense danger, they go into high gear, ready for any encounter. And when they strike, the first blow goes straight to the heart. Scorpios are strong, both spiritually and physically, and are endowed with the willpower to attain whatever goals they set for themselves. They are extremely independent. Scorpios do not feel comfortable unless they are in control and have the upper hand. Their determination is rivaled only by their impatience.

According to the *Book of Formation*, every zodiac sign is associated with a particular part of the human body. It should come as no surprise that the region related to Scorpio is that of the sexual organs, the portion of the anatomy that so powerfully influences human behavior. Scorpios of both genders are often deemed "sexy," but both can easily become destructive in the use of their sexual power.

Scorpios love melodramatic stories, and are gratified by extreme emotions. While they yearn for love and adore grand gestures, they do not like to display their need for love. Their jealousy is legendary; they simply cannot stand to see someone else with something that they want. Their envy is all the more dangerous because it expresses itself subtly. Scorpios love to work in secret. They are most discrete in their negative behavior when their *Desire to Receive* is at its highest. Scorpios can become so consumed by envy that they shower their unsuspecting victims with negativity. Having a Scorpio as an enemy can be devastating.

Scorpios are not very logical, but they are highly intuitive and can detect the innermost feelings of others. They immediately discern other people's weaknesses and will not hesitate to reveal them openly.

Scorpios do not lie, either to themselves or to others, and are unburdened by any form of tact. If you want to find out about yourself, particularly your worst aspects, simply ask a Scorpio! Although Scorpios can be profoundly generous and giving, they usually seek to make the receiver dependent and subordinate. Their giving is not sharing in the true sense, since it is performed only to gain control.

Scorpios want desperately to be in control, yet they are dominated by their emotions, carried from one extreme feeling to another. They can change from blind love to fierce hate in no time at all. They easily blame their distress on others, and take out their anxieties on the people around them. And they never forget a slight. Anyone—family, friends, bank tellers—who has ever made them suffer will feel their sting. Scorpios may even be aware that their actions can have a boomerang effect—that one day they will receive exactly what they gave. But this does not stop them. What matters to a Scorpio is settling the score.

Kabbalah tells us that we have all come into this world for the purpose of carrying out our *tikkun*, our correction. In order to accomplish this, you can either become more spiritually aware or, through some external "twist of fate," you can be led to an understanding of your correct path. The universe, like any other community or country, has laws by which it is governed. While you have been given free will and the right to do as you please, you are an integral part of this universe and are subject to its laws.

The consequences of our actions are always waiting for us just around the corner. What goes around comes around.

Scorpio is a water sign, but in Kabbalah the sign is also very closely associated with fire. Scorpios are a living paradox: Water is the symbol of sharing and mercy, while fire is the symbol of judgment. The fire in Scorpios makes them impulsive. They have little patience, and they deny themselves time to think things through before they act. They become insensitive to others' needs. The healing, meaningful part of a Scorpio never gets a chance to emerge. Without mercy, judgment is cruel, harsh, and unfeeling. Scorpios have to temper their fire with water.

Scorpios must learn to detach from their emotions. Whenever you experience a surge of anger, passion, or hatred, you must endeavor to control it. Scorpios should stop manufacturing crises and dramas that eventually overwhelm them and those around them. **When Scorpios allow the water side of their characters to emerge, they can transform their nature and ascend to higher levels of consciousness.**

IF YOUR *TIKKUN* (CORRECTION) IS IN SCORPIO...

In your past life you were Taurus, the Bull. Firmly attached to a certain way of seeing the world, you were stubborn, slow, and extremely reluctant to change. Susceptible to bodily pleasures, you were a consummate hedonist. You were in love with beauty and nature, were extremely possessive, and pursued material rather than spiritual assets. Fearful of the loss of your own comfort, you cut yourself off from meaningful experiences. Your life has been routine and empty. Hemmed in by obstinacy, you neither listened to nor learned from others. But this time you have what it takes to achieve genuine transformation.

Now you need to abandon the rigid rules that marked your previous life and allow spontaneity to enter, tasting freedom of action. This way you will become aware of the illusions that burdened your spirit, trusting the Light to protect you. In this way, you will prove yourself worthy of respect and love.

This could prove to be a difficult correction. It might cause some painful material losses. Initially, your comfort, your sense of security, may feel threatened. If you want to accomplish your correction, however, you will have to pay the price. As time goes on, you will become more independent in your actions. Your relationships will deepen as you become more capable of empathy, as long as you start considering others differently—not for their material value, but for their worth as human beings. You might even discover an aptitude for psychology—your way of opening up to this world. Along this path, you can experience a beautiful karmic metamorphosis. **By letting go of your fear of loss, you can increase your capacity to receive, both spiritually and materially.**

THIS MONTH'S INFLUENCE ON ALL OF US:

Inner Negativity

A challenging month is upon us. Our negative traits and deep-rooted egocentric qualities rise to the forefront. Resist the compelling urge to react. Rise above the primitive power of impulse and discover what you truly need to correct in the course of your spiritual development.

THE MONTH OF *KISLEV* (SAGITTARIUS)

Like a Rainbow

The month of *Kislev* (Sagittarius) is the ninth month/sign in the lunar calendar and is ruled by the planet Jupiter, the planetary symbol of abundance, good luck, and good fortune.

The Aramaic letters connecting us to the spiritual aspects of the month/sign are *Samech* ⸂, which created the sign of Sagittarius, and *Gimel* ⸂, which created the planet Jupiter. *Samech* means encouragement, sustenance, or assistance, while *Gimel* means sharing. Together they suggest a month in which we find security, well-being, and hope, provided that we don't allow ourselves to slip into complacency and self-righteousness. All in all, this is considered an extremely positive month.

Sagittarius, *Keshet* in Aramaic, means rainbow, the seven basic colors that make up the spectrum of visible light. *The Zohar* tells us that the rainbow is the force that counterbalances judgment. In The Bible, the rainbow appeared in the heavens to signal the end of Noah's flood, a symbol of hope and new beginnings.

Sagittarius is a fire sign that is intimately associated with the element of air. This is taken to mean that Sagittarians are propelled by fire, like a rocket, by a force lying deep within their spirit. Because of this inner fire, Sagittarians constantly seek challenges and risks. As we will see, this daredevil quality has both good and bad effects.

Even as children, Sagittarians distinguish themselves from the rest of the group by constantly looking for new challenges. This adventurous behavior, if not balanced by good judgment, makes them somewhat irresponsible. Testing themselves is the only thing that interests them, and they will even go out of their way to make a particular test more difficult. If Sagittarians have an exam coming up, they will wait until the very last minute to study for it. Rather than causing anxiety, this added pressure brings out the best in them. Sagittarians need to feel pressure in order to succeed. The pressure nourishes them. Without it, they lose interest very quickly.

When an opportunity for adventure arises, Sagittarians rush in—the more impossible the task, the greater their enthusiasm. They seize every opportunity to perform heroically and are constantly striving to extend their own limits. It is no coincidence, then, that the organs of the body that relate to Sagittarians are the hips and the legs.

Sagittarians seek pleasure at almost any cost. They want instant gratification, and they derive it mostly from taking chances and facing their fears. Because of this, their thoughts and actions do not focus on the goal itself, but on the means of deriving maximum pleasure from the undertaking. Though intending no harm, they are preoccupied with proving themselves and can be insensitive to the doubts and fears of those around them. It is a point of honor to Sagittarians to take up any challenge they encounter, and they generally do so with a certain joyful exuberance. Should they fail, however, they are haunted by guilt and relive the event over and over.

Sagittarians are generally intelligent, or at least rational. They focus on essentials. They love to learn new things but dislike rigidity of any kind, and they tend to seek their education in unconventional settings. Sagittarians love freedom and cannot stay in one place for very long; they prefer to explore new horizons, both physical and intellectual. This wanderlust applies to relationships as well. Sagittarians periodically need to "rediscover" their partners. If they feel a routine setting into their relationship, it becomes difficult for them to stay.

Sagittarians are uncompromising and extremely critical of their own behavior. To their credit, they always look for the fault in themselves and immediately take full responsibility for their actions and mistakes. Sagittarians never put the blame on others. Furthermore, they do not hold grudges, are not resentful, are quick to forgive and may even become fixated on their own inadequacies and failures.

Each and every mistake that Sagittarians make is engraved in their memories for future reference. Though too proud to admit it, Sagittarians do listen to criticism. They learn from it and use it in making their *tikkun*, their correction. They even learn from their friends' mistakes, and integrate these experiences into their own development. They see everything as an opportunity to learn and progress.

According to *The Zohar*, the rainbow is an energy field that appears whenever a decree of destruction has been issued. Its role is to ward off disaster and help protect us. For Sagittarians, the rainbow sign is a shield on which they depend. Sagittarians experience miracles throughout their lives; in fact, they come to expect them. For Sagittarians, there is always a "happy ending." The influence of Jupiter convinces them that everything will be fine in the end. While Kabbalah teaches us that this is ultimately true, Sagittarians must not allow their optimism to become complacency and smugness. They cannot simply depend on the planetary influence to pull them through their correction. Everyone has work to do.

Sagittarians need to stop looking at every challenge as an opportunity for enjoyment and take up the great spiritual challenge of revealing the Light. To avoid acting irresponsibly, you should restrict your adventurous behavior. You must learn that everything you seek is already here, that the only true goal is to do good and reveal the Light. Since Kabbalah tells us that we are given only those tasks or tests that we are already capable of fulfilling, we cannot take any credit for their accomplishment. **We are not the source; the Light is the source.**

Sagittarian correction is quite easily attainable, since Sagittarians naturally strive to progress, learn, and control their own destinies. As soon as they are confronted with a problem, they search for a way to solve it. They accept the discomfort in order to stretch themselves, and this is precisely the way to self-improvement and correction.

IF YOUR *TIKKUN* (CORRECTION) IS IN
SAGITTARIUS...

If your *tikkun* is in Sagittarius, you retain the duality that characterized your previous incarnation as a Gemini. Having always considered your life from two opposing viewpoints, you lived with deep uncertainty. Decision making was your major obstacle. You could not establish a definite course of action and stick to it. One of your problems in past lives and early in this life was a lack of concentration, which made you appear superficial. Your instability hindered your effort to attain professional standing and handicapped your spiritual and physical evolution. To be accepted in a group, you danced to any tune. Because of this chameleon-like tendency, you were often called a hypocrite.

Your *tikkun* in Sagittarius challenges you to define your aims and accomplish them. Your responsibilities and obligations are opportunities to solidify your own opinions. You can turn your back on your superficial past and finally confront reality. You bridge this transformation through loyalty. In fact, **you will be so eager for justice that integrity, sincerity, and a**

refusal to compromise will become central issues in your evolution.

You can find your own identity—authenticity will be at the heart of your commitment—and discover your true mission on earth: sharing your wisdom and revealing truth.

THIS MONTH'S INFLUENCE ON
ALL OF US:

Miracles

The Aramaic word for miracles, *nes*, also means to "run away." When we "run away" from the *Desire to Receive for the Self Alone*—the selfish longings of our ego—miracles happen. In other words, we must affect the miracle within nature in order to ignite miracles around us. Your ability to transform from a place of reactivity to one of sharing will determine the amount of miracles that you'll witness in this month.

THE MONTH OF *TEVET* (CAPRICORN)

Living in the Material World

Tevet is the tenth month on the Aramaic calendar and is ruled by the planet Saturn. Of the five inner planets created by the Aramaic letters, Saturn is the farthest from the sun. Because of this distance, Kabbalah tells us that Capricorn is the sign that most nurtures delusions.

The month of Capricorn is a very spiritual month. The planet Saturn was created by the letter *Bet* **ב**, and Capricorn was created by the letter *Ayin* **ע**. Together, these two letters link us directly to the 72 channels of energy through which Light descends into the world. They also connect to the element of water, which is a symbol of mercy.

Capricorn is an earth sign, and Capricorns are often somewhat slow and heavy in their demeanor. They are usually reserved and not very talkative; it takes them a while to warm up and smile. Capricorns often have a bony look, and their appearance is very grounded. Is it any wonder that the organs of the body that correspond to Capricorns are the skin and the bones? They usually prefer their own company to a busy social life—just like hermits. Capricorns are deeply attached to the physical realm in which the *Desire to Receive* manifests itself.

From an early age, Capricorns feel they have to assume responsibility. Often they prematurely abandon their dreams to face the cold realities of adulthood. Because of this, in later years they may feel they were deprived of something. They are generally serious people and do not give of themselves readily. In their minds, people are responsible for their own lives. To a Capricorn, everything has to be earned—there are no "free lunches." In short, Capricorns have a very matter-of-fact and often uncharitable view of the world.

Sefer Yetzirah, the *Book of Formation*, describes Saturn's inner spiritual energy as dry and cold. Perhaps this is why Capricorns find it hard to express their feelings or to give or receive love. This lack of warmth is present throughout the lives of many Capricorns, though they keep it buried deep within their souls.

Capricorns are the most materialistic sign of the zodiac. All their thoughts and feelings tend to be connected to physical matter. They have strong analytical skills and make excellent business people and scientists. Capricorns are independent and do not tolerate authority. Their determination helps them attain a certain social standing, which they are constantly trying to improve. They are very demanding, both of themselves and of others. They are reliable but move forward slowly, step by step, in order to protect themselves. They are very practical, always trying to keep busy in order to remain one step ahead of the competition. A Capricorn knows that achievement in any area takes both hard work and perseverance.

Capricorns' two governing values are time and money, both of which are precious to them. Having worked so hard to obtain what they want, they believe they are entitled to everything they get. They have an overdeveloped sense of ownership and are extremely protective of their possessions. They are highly averse to risk for fear of losing what they have worked so hard to attain. Capricorns tend to be unsympathetic to anyone who appears to receive things without working as hard as they have.

Capricorn represents midheaven—the highest point in the firmament. From this vantage point, Capricorns can see both the spiritual and material purposes of life. Unfortunately, they seldom take full advantage of their unique perspective. Capricorns usually come down on the material side of things, but the potential for seeing the spiritual dimension is always present.

We are all made up of physical matter and spirit, body and soul, a beautiful combination of the physical and the metaphysical. Kabbalah teaches us that it is a mistake to remain attached to only one of these two worlds to the exclusion of the other.

From this, we can begin to discern a positive direction that Capricorns can take toward making their necessary correction and elevating the level of their souls. Making this correction is not easy. But as we have said, where the potential for negativity is highest, there is also the greatest potential for manifestation of the Light.

Saturn's coldness is associated with its distance from the sun. In Kabbalah, the sun links us to the Infinite Light, the spiritual energy that created us. But Capricorns are bound to matter and its limitations. Feeling cut off from the spiritual energy of the sun, Capricorns invest their energy in the material world. In fact, the material world may often seem to be the only world available to them.

But the Creator would not present us with an obstacle that we could not transcend. Kabbalah teaches us that Capricorn is an earth sign that is intimately associated with the element of water, which represents the quality of mercy. Though the Light is blocked, distant, or filtered, the potential for receiving blessing is still there.

These spiritual notions are not alien to Capricorns. They have enormous spiritual potential, provided that they want to develop it.

Capricorns need to understand that everything they have acquired in the physical world is not as a result of their personal merit, hard work, or determination; the source of all these things is the Light. Kabbalah teaches us that the material outcome of any endeavor is, in fact, of little importance. What matters is a combination of the way we accomplish our correction and our motivation for wanting to do so. Capricorns should understand that if they confine their desires to material things, they will remain unsatisfied and frustrated.

When you become stuck in the delusions of the physical world, you begin to believe that things "belong" to you, that somehow these things are fundamentally "yours." But Capricorns must share. **The more you share, the more energy you reveal and the more accomplished you feel. Sharing helps Capricorns reveal their true nature, which is sensitive and humane.**

By turning your determination and perseverance to the service of others, you will develop new and satisfying spiritual abilities. You will come to understand that work is an opportunity to reveal good, and not drudgery attached to an eventual material reward.

IF YOUR *TIKKUN* (CORRECTION) IS IN CAPRICORN...

D oubts inherited from a previous life can burden the person whose *tikkun* is in Capricorn. Having endured the influence of Cancer, you deal with being constantly anxious. Throughout your past life, you sought security to the extent that you idealized life. In this way, you managed either to conceal your problems or to eagerly accept the direction of others, thereby rejecting every kind of responsibility.

As a consequence, you are the ultimate conformist. You may never really have opened up to the possibilities of the outside world. You may live as a hermit, buried in your own world, relying on materialism for your security. You avoid any true connections with people or ideas. Owing to your lack of self-confidence, you curtail your experiences and force yourself to stay unhealthily close to your family, particularly your parents. Because of this, you unfairly make them the scapegoat for all your weaknesses. You have been marked by your father's image and had to start your life with this handicap.

You could have transferred this regard and effort to society as a whole.

In the past you refused to grow and acted in an infantile manner, never taking risks. In order to achieve security, you organized your life according to the rules and laws of society, which could have made you a patriot or at least a politician.

A correction in Capricorn will teach you maturity. You will have to cut the umbilical cord with family. You will have to accept your responsibilities and also look for new ones to dispel your anxieties. In this way, you will taste the pleasures of risk taking. You will enjoy committing yourself without forethought. Find a worthy cause and identify with it, and you will be able to draw on your inner strength to face up to obstacles. You will gain self-mastery and readiness to fulfill your spiritual mission in life.

THIS MONTH'S INFLUENCE ON
ALL OF US:

Control

To gain control, we must relinquish control. Therein is the ultimate paradox of this month. Be extra conscious that you do not act alone. Be more aware that you are a part of a master plan that includes the rest of the people in this universe. Resist those seductive thoughts telling you that you are the center of the universe, the master of your domain. Realize that you're part of a larger picture. This enlightened consciousness will prevent your impure actions from hurting others, and allow your positive actions to increase the radiance of Light in this world.

THE MONTH OF *SHVAT* (AQUARIUS)

Under Water

The Month of *Shvat* is the eleventh month of the lunar year and is ruled by Saturn. In Aramaic, Aquarius is *D'li*, meaning bucket or pitcher, and the sign is represented by a water bearer pouring water. As we know, water is the symbol of mercy and purification. Aquarius is both the channel for appeasing the world and the sign of abundance; everything is poured out and shared, with no accounting.

The letters of the month of *Shvat* are *Bet* ⊐, which created Saturn, and *Tzadi* ⊻, which created the sign of Aquarius. The letter *Bet* symbolizes centrality; it manifests equilibrium and balance and is also the force of benediction or approval. The letter *Tzadi* means "just," which indicates equilibrium. During this period, we are given the opportunity to reveal truth and light. Because of this, the month of *Shvat* is considered the Month of Redemption.

Aquarius follows Capricorn in the zodiac cycle and is also ruled by Saturn. Does having the same ruling planet imply that these two signs possess similar qualities? Not really, and here's why. If we look closely at Saturn, we see that one aspect faces back into the solar system toward the sun, while the other faces out to the infinity of space. The former aspect influences Capricorn, while the latter affects Aquarius. Whereas a Capricorn is faced with *limitation*, an Aquarius is faced with *infinity*. This causes the two signs to have almost diametrically opposed characteristics. While Capricorns spend their lives building structures and systems, Aquarians spend their lives tearing them down.

Aquarians are unique. You can't ignore them. As children, they show great promise. As adults, they are idealists who strive to change the universe through original thinking. They are rebels with many causes; their concern is for the well-being of humanity as a whole.

Though Aquarians seek justice for all, this quest is at a global level, not a personal one. They support grand and noble causes but often fail to help those who are suffering nearby. They prefer to deal with the social rights of an entire nation rather than with the problems of those close to them. Two reasons underlie this apparent contradiction: First, Aquarians generally lack a sense of the practical; and second, Aquarians are passionately independent and private. Driven by their yearning for originality, they set themselves apart from the crowd.

Despite their friendliness and open-mindedness, Aquarians are the most stubborn of all signs. They reject all established structures. Whether in marriage or in business, Aquarians fight to maintain their individuality and freedom in order to exercise their innovative ideas. They detest containment and destroy all limitations that may lie in their paths. Theoretically, **Aquarians are here to break down structures and systems, to demolish walls. However, the thickest walls they encounter are often those of their own egos.** Even when they do start to make changes in their lives, Aquarians tend to focus their attention outside, remaining unchanged deep within their hearts. The body element that relates to and is affected by Aquarius is the blood.

According to kabbalists, our present era started about 400 years ago and is variously called the Age of Aquarius, the Age of Revelation, or the Age of Redemption. Why does Aquarius symbolize redemption? Because Aquarians perceive the world as unified and kabbalists consider this to be the basis of true redemption. Redemption is the moment when all negativity is cleansed, when humanity is free of evil and fragmentation. Because of their higher level of consciousness, Aquarians are directly linked to this redemptive moment.

In Kabbalah, the New Year of the Plant Kingdom is celebrated on the 15th day of the month of Aquarius, *Tu Bishvat*, because of the powerful energy that is manifested during this time. Vegetation is the only force in the physical world that seems able to overcome the force of gravity, which in Kabbalah is the most powerful expression of the *Desire to Receive*. Like trees and plants, Aquarians have the power to break through the constraints of the physical world.

But in order to make this power manifest, Aquarians must control the aspects of their nature that interfere with its accomplishment. To understand how to control the nature of a particular sign, kabbalistic astrology often looks at its opposite. On the astrological map, the sign opposite Aquarius is Leo. Leo is "the king," while Aquarius is "the people." This tells us that **Aquarians certainly are capable of helping humanity, as long as their own ideas do not become more important than the cause itself.**

Aquarians must learn that caring about society does not mean neglecting the individual. True spirituality means being part of humanity, not above it. Unfortunately, Aquarians usually have such high opinions of themselves that imposing their own views can become their sole objective. Aquarians must conquer their boundless pride. Neither your ideas nor your energy are of your own making. You have been entrusted with these attributes in order to manifest a certain force in this world. You are merely channels for this energy and therefore are not entitled to personal glory.

For the rest of us, the month of *Shvat* offers the opportunity to free ourselves from our restrictions and connect to the infinite. We live in the Age of Aquarius, a time when incredible innovations have become an integral part of daily life. If Aquarians are spiritual, it is because time has no hold on them. They conceive of the future as already here; they have only to reveal it. All of us can use the influence of this month to aspire to the same attitudes.

IF YOUR *TIKKUN* (CORRECTION) IS IN AQUARIUS...

You are a true monarch, returning to the physical realm to correct pride left over from your previous incarnation as a Leo. In your last incarnation, you dominated your subjects. You lived in the limelight. You loved flashiness and luxury, and as a result you will not find it easy to do without. Moreover, overcoming your pride will not be the obvious thing to do, since pride has been reinforced in previous reincarnations.

The *tikkun* in Aquarius will make you face difficulties in your marriage—namely, accepting a partner as an equal with whom to share everything. This is the preliminary "drill" to overcoming your pride. At the outset of your present incarnation, you still sought the admiration to which you were formerly accustomed. You arrogantly exploited your power to control others. Considering yourself the center of the universe was your way of expressing a need for love and gratitude. You had to struggle to discern reality. Having lived in an artificial world, you had great difficulty finding a spiritual path. As one used to ruling over your subjects, climbing down does not come naturally to you.

A *tikkun* in Aquarius engenders certain obstacles in relationships. In marriage, for example, you must slowly but surely abandon your preoccupation with your own selfish desires. You will have to exchange your sacrosanct independence for a new concept: interdependence. This world is not "me" versus all others; we are all equal on the same level. If you give up honor and glamour, you will succeed in creating an immense restriction and take control of the duality of your correction—your personal life and your humanitarian mission.

The *tikkun* in Aquarius is, in fact, that of the true missionary. You can attain the consciousness of a cosmic reality and feel responsible for humanity as a whole. You can know true friendship and perhaps even universal fraternity. Having inherited a leonine power, you have the strength to accomplish this task. Utilize it for the benefit of all. You can experience an exceptional and unique adventure in the history of humanity if you manage the most difficult restriction: silencing your ego and practicing humility and modesty while living in simplicity.

THIS MONTH'S INFLUENCE ON
ALL OF US:

Letting Go

Shvat arouses an abundance of Light, and for that reason, *The Zohar* reveals that the final redemption will take place in the age and month of Aquarius. Let go of your negativity and you will receive an equal measure of pure Light in return. Hanging onto to our ego, opinions, bad habits, and other self-indulgences will cause us to miss the myriad of opportunities for spiritual connections that occur in this Light-filled month.

THE MONTH OF *ADAR* (PISCES)

Born to Share

*A*dar is the twelfth and last month on the lunar calendar. In Aramaic, *Adar* signifies the spine and spinal
cord that holds together the entire body. In a similar
manner, Pisces is considered the month that stabilizes the
months/signs of the zodiac. Without Pisces, the zodiac would
fall apart.

As the last sign, Pisces reveals the sum total of all that preceded
it. Because of this, during the month of Pisces we can take
control of the entire year. It is a month surrounded by the
positive energy of water and protected by the abundance and
good fortune of Jupiter.

The Aramaic letters that connect us to the positive aspects of
the month of Adar are *Kuf* ק, which created Pisces, and
Gimel ג, which created the planet Jupiter. *Gimel* means
"sharing." Kabbalah considers the letter *Kuf* to be a sort of
double agent. It is the only letter in the Aramaic alphabet
to go below the writing line, symbolizing a link to the

World Below, the World of Illusion. It is thought, however, that while *Kuf* serves to feed the negativity and appears to be an agent of negativity, it is actually an agent of the Light. For this and many other reasons, *Adar* is known as the Month of Joy.

Pisces is a water sign. More than that, it represents the power of "balanced" waters. Pisceans therefore have two sources of protection: one from the planet Jupiter (justice and equilibrium) and the other from the purity of water (mercy).

It is said that great spirits, who have very little correction left to do, reincarnate as Pisceans.

Probably as a consequence of this abundance of gifts, Pisces is the humblest sign of the zodiac and naturally yields to others. Pisceans are extremely sensitive; they feel the vibrations and emotions of events unfolding around them. Furthermore, in their desire to eliminate other people's suffering, they take pain upon themselves, enduring suffering and problems as though they were their own. As the last sign of the zodiac, Pisces represents the sphere of *Malchut*, or manifestation. Because of this, Pisces is the sign with responsibility for all the others.

For this reason, people love to confide in Pisceans, knowing they will find comfort and support. But it is important for Pisceans to remember that they cannot really help anyone if they allow their sensitivity to gain the upper hand. They must remember that sometimes it is essential to tell others what is wrong so that they may confront their problems as the first step toward correction. Too often, Pisceans will mistakenly let their compassion cloud the truth.

In Aramaic, Pisces is called *Dagim*, which means "fishes." The letters of this word refer to a uniquely Piscean concept: *Gomel Dalim*, meaning "help the poor." This is why Pisceans can be humble, gentle, kind, altruistic, and ready to give everything they have. They do not desire anything for themselves.

One of the problems faced by Pisceans is their *Desire to Receive***, or their lack thereof.** Pisceans are satisfied with what they have and who they are. If and when they do have a desire for something more, or for something difficult to obtain, Pisceans may sometimes lack the spiritual wherewithal to fight for it. More than any other sign, Pisceans know that in the end, everything will be fine. They are well aware that everything in this world is an illusion—that everything has already been decided, and that the suffering of this world is only temporary. So why struggle? After all, life is only a game, and the dice have already been cast. This passive, reactive perception of the world often condemns Pisceans to a complacent life, like fish in an aquarium—one in which all their needs are met.

But Pisceans have not been put on this earth to simply sit back and let things happen. **They need to be reminded that their reason for being here is to manifest the Light, and that without action, no Light can be revealed.**

Certain signs of the zodiac are pairs, such as Gemini and Libra, and their duality stems from the nature of their symbol. But why is the sign of Pisces always represented by two fish swimming in opposite directions? This is because Pisceans are connected to two worlds: physicality, because they are human; and spirituality, because they have evolved in a different sphere of consciousness. Pisceans can pass from one world to the other, grasping the spirit behind matter while also concretizing matter in spirit.

Kabbalistic astrology tells us that Aries is the first sign of the zodiac. Since it is, so to speak, the first in line, it does not see other months and is therefore the sign with the greatest *Desire to Receive for the Self Alone*. Pisces, however, is the last sign of the zodiac cycle. It is the one sign for whom sharing comes naturally. In their hearts, Pisceans know that service and devotion to their fellow creatures is the purpose of life.

Because of this, Pisceans have true potential to accomplish their correction on earth, depending on the work they do on themselves. But if Pisceans believe that their *tikkun* will be accomplished simply because they lack a *Desire to Receive for the Self Alone*, they may be surprised to learn that they are wrong. This perception is their Achilles heel. In fact, Pisceans need to desire *more*—not for themselves but for humanity. They must take action to see that needs are met and problems are rectified. Pisceans are connected to a spiritual frequency that enables them to know what they must do, but they must choose the means. Knowing what is concealed from others is not enough; **revealing what is concealed is the true work of Pisceans.**

IF YOUR *TIKKUN* (CORRECTION) IS IN PISCES...

The *tikkun* in Pisces deals mainly with the conscious perception of another dimension. Your previous life as a Virgo has left you with an inability to detach yourself from logic; you think and live in a reasonable world. Though this life shows you other viewpoints, in your previous incarnation you could not "see the forest for the trees." You were absorbed in intricate rationalizations that, although right in the beginning, did not satisfy you in the end because you saw only one side of the picture (the physical one). Your concern for details turned you into an irascible and fussy person. Having fallen into excessive organizing, you lost all trace of spontaneity.

This leftover Virgo behavior has also led to difficulties and disagreements in your sexual life. Your unwillingness to get emotionally involved, coupled with your fear of not being able to control a relationship, led you to forbid yourself emotional outbursts of any kind. Very rigid in your way of thinking, you were incapable of listening and learning from others.

By demanding factual perfection in your previous life, you made your task more difficult than it would otherwise have been. You aimed too high and lost your self-confidence. In your efforts to understand and master your own life, everything was compartmentalized and labeled according to strict rules. But existence does not conform to Descartes. Having fragmented your previous life, you are now stuck with the problem of how to put the pieces back together in this one.

The *tikkun* in Pisces suggests that you must first understand that you cannot perceive the essence of truth through your senses, but that a spiritual reality is the origin of everything physical. Give up analyzing the effect and you will perceive the cause. Abandoning your need for logical explanations will enable you to erase the doubts that have plagued you for so long. Along this path, you will gain an image of the world that goes beyond the senses and opens the door to a more spiritual level of consciousness.

Here you can experience emotions that will help you change your perception of others; by judging them less, they will offer you more. This will ignite within you a love for your fellow beings and reinforce your compassion. In this way, you will learn how to act on two levels: You can live in the present while looking into the future. **Acting in the moment to serve a universal mission in which you have faith is the key to achieving a true rebirth and attaining universal consciousness.**

THIS MONTH'S INFLUENCE ON ALL OF US:

Happiness

The more we engage in the pursuit of happiness to fill our own desires, the more elusive joy will be. Likewise, the more we dedicate ourselves to bringing happiness to others, the more joy will rain down upon us from the heavens above. This is the paradoxical power of *Adar*. This month, focus on bringing happiness to others so that you will receive happiness yourself.

ACRUX

BETA CRUCIS

AGENA

RIGIL K

SPICA

ANTARES

NOV

FORGOTTEN
INFLUENCES

I t is written in *The Zohar* that the wisdom of Kabbalah would have to wait for the coming of the Age of Enlightenment (Age of Aquarius) to make its reappearance as a tool for humankind to draw down the Light upon the human race.

That age has arrived!

Today, more than any other time in history, the opportunity to use the wisdom of Kabbalah in our everyday lives is a reality. What was once an esoteric and hidden discipline known only to a few scholars is now available to the masses—people like you and me. With this book, we have attempted to explain, in an easily understandable way, the origins of Kabbalah, its basic principles, and how we can use those principles with the conventional 12 signs of the zodiac to regain control of our lives. But if this book has been at all successful, it should now be clear as well that at its core, kabbalistic wisdom contains a very simple and vastly more important message.

Kabbalah tells us that the world we live in is the seeable, touchable, hearable, smellable, and tastable form of an indescribably beautiful and endlessly enduring spiritual world. It teaches that we—you, me, your Aunt Millie—are the links between this physical world and all the spiritual worlds above. Most importantly, Kabbalah tells us that we have been placed here in order to share, and by sharing, become more like the infinite positive Light by which and of which we are made.

Learning about the stars and planets is simply a tool to help us attain this ultimate goal—to become more like the Light that made us.

This book then, is a tool. It allows us to use the kabbalistic understanding of the spiritual nature of the universe for our own purpose, and to help us make the necessary corrections in our lives that will give us the best chance at success, both spiritual and physical. Through an understanding of our relationship with the Upper Worlds, and an awareness of our unbreakable connection with the spiritual dimensions of the universe, as well as an appreciation of the possibilities and opportunities presented to us by the positions of the stars and planets, we can take control of our destiny and become proactive, positive, and, above all, sharing forces in the world.

Finally, it is important to say one more thing. As we mentioned earlier, Kabbalah teaches us that we are "free agents." Our fate, our destiny, is in our own hands. There is never a moment when we do not have a choice to make, and there is never a choice that is inconsequential or meaningless. At every point in our lives, we are deciding our destiny.

Some of these decisions may seem to affect only ourselves, but most of the decisions that we make will have consequences that influence the lives of others—perhaps even having far-reaching effects on the world. The question most of us have is, "How do we identify those choices that will have positive consequences and protect ourselves from making choices that do not?"

As we hope this book has made clear, Kabbalah teaches us that **if we focus our attention on making choices with the ultimate goal is sharing or giving, we will be going a long way toward always making a choice that will have a positive effect—lifting our consciousness, and allowing us to become more like the Light that made us.**

Through Kabbalah, we learn that each constellation, each month of the year, every moment in time presents us with its own unique opportunity to choose a path that can have a positive effect on our own consciousness as well as on society as a whole. By taking the opportunity to share in a thousand different ways, we open ourselves up to receiving a positive, rejuvenating energy to fill us up again. Remember, the more room we make in the Vessel, the more Light is required to fill it up again.

We hope you will use this book to expand your own Vessel and generate spiritual Light both personally and for all people on this planet.

INFLUENCE OF PAST LIFETIMES

According to Kabbalah, our astral chart contains a position that unveils the secrets of our previous lifetimes: the lunar node, the point of correction—*tikkun*. This position comprises two diametrically opposing aspects that conventional astrology calls the south node and the north node. The point of correction brings to light the barriers that have been buried deep within us through the ages.

The study of this point reveals the challenges and blockages we perpetually face, the nature of our impediments, and the aspects we must correct in order to pursue our personal evolution and seek a superior and more elevated consciousness. If we fail to undertake serious spiritual work during our present incarnation, we will inevitably return to the same process and again face the same obstacles. This point shows us our weaknesses as well as the groundwork on which we must build our future. Thanks to this tool, we have the ability to recognize the baggage we have brought along from previous incarnations and thus master its effects.

TIKKUN REFERENCE TABLE

If you were born between these two dates:	Your point of *tikkun* is:
22 January 1901 to 21 July 1902	Scorpio
22 July 1902 to 15 January 1904	Libra
16 January 1904 to 18 September 1905	Virgo
19 September 1905 to 30 March 1907	Leo
31 March 1907 to 27 September 1908	Cancer
28 September 1908 to 23 March 1910	Gemini
24 March 1910 to 8 December 1911	Taurus
9 December 1911 to 6 June 1913	Aries
7 June 1913 to 3 December 1914	Pisces
4 December 1914 to 31 May 1916	Aquarius
1 June 1916 to 13 February 1918	Capricorn
14 February 1918 to 15 August 1919	Sagittarius
16 August 1919 to 7 February 1921	Scorpio
8 February 1921 to 23 August 1922	Libra
24 August 1922 to 23 April 1924	Virgo
24 April 1924 to 26 October 1925	Leo
27 October 1925 to 16 April 1927	Cancer
17 April 1927 to 28 December 1928	Gemini
29 December 1928 to 7 July 1930	Taurus
8 July 1930 to 28 December 1931	Aries
29 December 1931 to 24 June 1933	Pisces
25 June 1933 to 8 March 1935	Aquarius
9 March 1935 to 14 September 1936	Capricorn
15 September 1936 to 3 March 1938	Sagittarius

4 March 1938 to 12 September 1939	Scorpio
13 September 1939 to 24 May 1941	Libra
25 May 1941 to 21 November 1942	Virgo
22 November 1942 to 11 May 1944	Leo
12 May 1944 to 13 December 1945	Cancer
14 December 1945 to 2 August 1947	Gemini
3 August 1947 to 26 January 1949	Taurus
27 January 1949 to 26 July 1950	Aries
27 July 1950 to 28 March 1952	Pisces
29 March 1952 to 9 October 1953	Aquarius
10 October 1953 to 2 April 1955	Capricorn
3 April 1955 to 4 October 1956	Sagittarius
5 October 1956 to 16 June 1958	Scorpio
17 June 1958 to 15 December 1959	Libra
16 December 1959 to 10 June 1961	Virgo
11 June 1961 to 23 December 1962	Leo
24 December 1962 to 25 August 1964	Cancer
26 August 1964 to 19 February 1966	Gemini
20 February 1966 to 19 August 1967	Taurus
20 August 1967 to 19 April 1969	Aries
20 April 1969 to 2 November 1970	Pisces
3 November 1970 to 27 April 1972	Aquarius
28 April 1972 to 27 October 1973	Capricorn
28 October 1973 to 10 July 1975	Sagittarius
11 July 1975 to 7 January 1977	Scorpio
8 January 1977 to 5 July 1978	Libra
6 July 1978 to 12 January 1980	Virgo
13 January 1980 to 24 September 1981	Leo
25 September 1981 to 16 March 1983	Cancer
17 March 1983 to 11 September 1984	Gemini

12 September 1984 to 6 April 1986	Taurus
7 April 1986 to 2 December 1987	Aries
3 December 1987 to 22 May 1989	Pisces
23 May 1989 to 18 November 1990	Aquarius
19 November 1990 to 1 August 1992	Capricorn
2 August 1992 to 1 February 1994	Sagittarius
2 February 1994 to 31 July 1995	Scorpio
1 August 1995 to 25 January 1997	Libra
26 January 1997 to 20 October 1998	Virgo
21 October 1998 to 9 April 2000	Leo
10 April 2000 to 12 October 2001	Cancer
13 October 2001 to 13 April 2003	Gemini
14 April 2003 to 25 December 2004	Taurus
26 December 2004 to 21 June 2006	Aries
22 June 2006 to 18 December 2007	Pisces
19 December 2007 to 21 August 2009	Aquarius
22 August 2009 to 3 March 2011	Capricorn
4 March 2011 to 29 August 2012	Sagittarius
30 August 2012 to 18 February 2014	Scorpio
19 February 2014 to 11 November 2015	Libra
12 November 2015 to 9 May 2017	Virgo
10 May 2017 to 6 November 2018	Leo
7 November 2018 to 4 May 2020	Cancer
5 May 2020 to 18 January 2022	Gemini
19 January 2022 to 17 July 2023	Taurus
18 July 2023 to 11 January 2025	Aries
12 January 2025 to 26 July 2026	Pisces
27 July 2026 to 26 March 2028	Aquarius
27 March 2028 to 23 September 2029	Capricorn

24 September 2029 to 20 March 2031	Sagittarius
21 March 2031 to 1 December 2032	Scorpio
2 December 2032 to 3 June 2034	Libra
4 June 2034 to 29 November 2035	Virgo
30 November 2035 to 29 May 2037	Leo
30 May 2037 to 9 February 2039	Cancer
10 February 2039 to 10 August 2040	Gemini
11 August 2040 to 3 February 2042	Taurus
4 February 2042 to 18 August 2043	Aries
19 August 2043 to 18 April 2045	Pisces
19 April 2045 to 18 October 2046	Aquarius
19October 2046 to11 April 2048	Capricorn
12 April 2048 to 14 December 2049	Sagittarius
15 December 2049 to 28 June 2051	Scorpio

Kabbalah Centre Books

72 Names of God, The: Technology for the Soul
72 Names of God for Kids, The: A Treasury of Timeless Wisdom
72 Names of God Meditation Book, The
And You Shall Choose Life: An Essay on Kabbalah, the Purpose of
    Life, and Our True Spiritual Work
Angel Intelligence: How Your Consciousness Determines Which Angels
    Come Into Your Life
AstrologiK: Kabbalistic Astrology Guide for Children
Becoming Like God: Kabbalah and Our Ultimate Destiny
Beloved of My Soul: Letters of Our Master and Teacher Rav Yehuda
    Tzvi Brandwein to His Beloved Student, Kabbalist Rav Berg
Consciousness and the Cosmos (Previously Star Connection)
Days of Connection: A Guide to Kabbalah's Holidays and New Moons
Days of Power Part 1
Days of Power Part 2
Dialing God: Daily Connection Book
Education of a Kabbalist
Energy of the Hebrew Letters, The (Previously Power of the Aleph
    Beth Vols. *1 and 2*)
Fear is Not an Option
Finding the Light Through the Darkness: Inspirational Lessons
    Rooted in the Bible and the Zohar
God Wears Lipstick: Kabbalah for Women
Holy Grail, The: A Manifesto on the Zohar
If You Don't Like Your Life, Change It!: Using Kabbalah to Rewrite the
    Movie of Your Life
Immortality: The Inevitability of Eternal Life
Kabbalah Connection, The: Preparing the Soul for Pesach
Kabbalah for the Layman
Kabbalah Method, The: The Bridge Between Science and the Soul,
    Physics and Fulfillment, Quantum and the Creator
Kabbalah On The Sabbath: Elevating Our Soul to the Light
Kabbalah: The Power To Change Everything
Kabbalistic Astrology: And the Meaning of Our Lives

Kabbalistic Bible: Genesis
Kabbalistic Bible: Exodus
Kabbalistic Bible: Leviticus
Kabbalistic Bible: Numbers
Kabbalistic Bible: Deuteronomy
Light of Wisdom: On Wisdom, Life, and Eternity
Miracles, Mysteries, and Prayer Volume 1
Miracles, Mysteries, and Prayer Volume 2
Nano: Technology of Mind Over Matter
Navigating The Universe: A Roadmap for Understanding the Cosmic
  Influences that Shape Our Lives (Previously Time Zones)
On World Peace: Two Essays by the Holy Kabbalist Rav Yehuda Ashlag
Path to the Light: Decoding the Bible with Kabbalah: Book of
  Beresheet Volume 1
Path to the Light: Decoding the Bible with Kabbalah: Book of
  Beresheet Volume 2
Path to the Light: Decoding the Bible with Kabbalah: Book of
  Beresheet Volume 3
Prayer of the Kabbalist, The: The 42-Letter Name of God
Power of Kabbalah, The: 13 Principles to Overcome Challenges and
  Achieve Fulfillment
Rebooting: Defeating Depression with the Power of Kabbalah
Satan: An Autobiography
Secret, The: Unlocking the Source of Joy & Fulfillment
Secrets of the Bible: Teachings from Kabbalistic Masters
Secrets of The Zohar: Stories and Meditations to Awaken the Heart
Simple Light: Wisdom from a Woman's Heart
Shabbat Connections
Taming Chaos: Harnessing the Secret Codes of the Universe to Make
  Sense of Our Lives
Thought of Creation, The: On the Individual, Humanity, and Their
  Ultimate Perfection
To Be Continued: Reincarnation & the Purpose of Our Lives
To the Power of One
True Prosperity: How to Have Everything
Vokabbalahry: Words of Wisdom for Kids to Live By
Way of the Kabbalist, The: A User's Guide To Technology for the Soul
Well of Life: Kabbalistic Wisdom from a Depth of Knowledge

Wheels of the Soul: Kabbalah and Reincarnation
Wisdom of Truth, The: 12 Essays by the Holy Kabbalist Rav Yehuda
Ashlag
Zohar, The

The *Zohar*

Composed more than 2,000 years ago, the 23-volume *Zohar* is a commentary on biblical and spiritual matters written in the form of conversations among teachers. It was given to all humankind by the Creator to bring us protection, to connect us with the Creator's Light, and ultimately to fulfill our birthright of transformation. The *Zohar* is an effective tool for achieving our purpose in life.

More than eighty years ago, when The Kabbalah Centre was founded, the *Zohar* had virtually disappeared from the world. Today, all this has changed. Through the editorial efforts of Michael Berg and The Kabbalah Centre, the *Zohar* is available in the original Aramaic language and for the first time in English with commentary.

We teach Kabbalah, not as a scholarly study but as a way of creating a better life and a better world.

WHO WE ARE

The Kabbalah Centre is a non-profit organization that makes the principles of Kabbalah understandable and relevant to everyday life. The Kabbalah Centre teachers provide students with spiritual tools based on kabbalistic principles that students can then apply as they see fit to improve their own lives and by doing so, make the world better. The Centre was founded by Rav Yehuda Ashlag in 1922 and now spans the globe with brick-and-mortar locations in more than 40 cities as well as an extensive online presence. To learn more, visit www.kabbalah.com.

WHAT WE TEACH

There are five core principles:

- **Sharing:** Sharing is the purpose of life and the only way to truly receive fulfillment. When individuals share, they connect to the force of energy that Kabbalah calls the Light—the Infinite Source of Goodness, the Divine Force, the Creator. By sharing, one can overcome ego—the force of negativity.

- **Awareness and Balance of the Ego:** The ego is a voice inside that directs people to be selfish, narrow-minded, limited, addicted, hurtful, irresponsible, negative, angry, and hateful. The ego is a main source of problems because it allows us to believe that others are separate from us. It is the opposite of sharing and humility. The ego also has a positive side, as it motivates one to take action. It is up to each individual to choose whether they act for themselves or whether to also act in the well-being of others. It is important to be aware of one's ego and to balance the positives and negatives.

- **Existence of Spiritual Laws:** There are spiritual laws in the universe that affect people's lives. One of these is the Law of Cause and Effect: What one puts out is what one get back, or what we sow is what we reap.

- **We Are All One:** Every human being has within him- or herself a spark of the Creator that binds each and every person into one totality. This understanding informs us of the spiritual precept that every human being must be treated with dignity at all times, under any circumstances. Individually, everyone is responsible for war and poverty in all parts of the world and individuals can't enjoy true and lasting fulfillment as long as others are suffering.

- **Leaving Our Comfort Zone Can Create Miracles:** Becoming uncomfortable for the sake of helping others taps us into a spiritual dimension that ultimately brings Light and positivity to our lives.

HOW WE TEACH

Courses and Classes. On a daily basis, The Kabbalah Centre focuses on a variety of ways to help students learn the core kabbalistic principles. For example, The Centre develops courses, classes, online lectures, books, and audio products. Online courses and lectures are critical for students located around the world who want to study Kabbalah but don't have access to a Kabbalah Centre in their community. To learn more, visit www.ukabbalah.com.

Spiritual Services and Events. The Centre organizes and hosts a variety of weekly and monthly events and spiritual services where students can participate in lectures, meditation and share meals together. Some events are held through live streaming online. The Centre organizes spiritual retreats and tours to energy sites, which are places that have been closely touched by great kabbalists. For example, tours take place at locations where kabbalists may have studied or been buried, or where ancient texts like the *Zohar* were authored. International events provide students from all over the world with an opportunity to make connections to unique energy available at certain times of the year. At these events, students meet with other students, share experiences and build friendships.

Volunteering. In the spirit of Kabbalah's principles that emphasize sharing, The Centre provides a volunteer program so that students can participate in charitable initiatives, which includes sharing the wisdom of Kabbalah itself through a mentoring program. Every year, hundreds of student volunteers organize projects that benefit their communities such as feeding the homeless, cleaning beaches and visiting hospital patients.

One-on-One. The Kabbalah Centre seeks to ensure that each student is supported in his or her study. Teachers and mentors are part of the educational infrastructure that is available to students 24 hours a day, seven days a week.

Hundreds of teachers are available worldwide for students as well as a study program for their continued development. Study takes place in person, by phone, in study groups, through webinars, and even self-directed study in audio format or online. To learn more visit, www.ukabbalah.com.

Publishing. Each year, The Centre translates and publishes some of the most challenging kabbalistic texts for advanced scholars including the *Zohar*, *Writings of the Ari*, and the *Ten Luminous Emanations with Commentary*. Drawing from these sources The Kabbalah Centre publishes books yearly in more than 30 languages that are tailored for both beginner- and intermediate-level students and distributed around the world.

Zohar Project. The *Zohar*, the primary text of kabbalistic wisdom, is a commentary on biblical and spiritual matters composed and compiled over 2000 years ago and is believed to be a source of Light. Kabbalists believe that when it is brought into areas of darkness and turmoil, the *Zohar* can create change and bring about improvement. The Kabbalah Centre's *Zohar* Project shares the *Zohar* in 30 countries by distributing free copies to organizations and individuals in recognition of their service to the community and to areas where there is danger. Since 2007, over 400,000 copies of the *Zohar* were donated to hospitals, embassies, places of worship, universities, not-for-profit organizations, emergency services, war zones, natural disaster locations, soldiers, pilots, government officials, medical professionals, humanitarian aid workers, and more.

In loving memory of our grandparents

Grisha, Pesach, Sonya, Chana, Moshe, Baruch, Rachel, Hannah

May the Light elevate and embrace their
souls with eternal blessings.